THE NATURE OF
SHOREBIRDS

THE NATURE OF

SHOREBIRDS

Nomads of the Wetlands

HARRY THURSTON

GREYSTONE BOOKS
Douglas & McIntyre
Vancouver/Toronto

Greystone Books
A division of Douglas & McIntyre Ltd.
1615 Venables Street
Vancouver, British Columbia V5L 2H1

Published in the United States of America by Sierra Club Books, San Francisco.

CANADIAN CATALOGUING IN PUBLICATION DATA

Thurston, Harry, 1950 –
    The nature of shorebirds

Includes bibliographical references and index.
ISBN 1-55054-502-7

1. Shore birds—North America. 2. Shore birds—North America—Migration. I. Title
QL696.C4T58 1996   598.3'3'097   C96-910081-7

Jacket and book design by DesignGeist
Editing by Anne Norman
Front jacket photograph by David Weintraub
Back jacket photograph by Art Wolfe
Printed and bound in China through Mandarin Offset

Pages ii–iii: Photograph by Arthur Morris / BIRDS AS ART
Page iv: Photograph by David Weintraub

The publisher gratefully acknowledges the assistance of the Canada Council and of the British
Columbia Ministry of Tourism, Small Business and Culture.

CONTENTS

ACKNOWLEDGEMENTS

The author would like to thank the many shorebird experts whose knowledge and generous spirit helped to inform and shape this book. I am grateful to Ian Davidson, Canada Program Manager, Wetlands for the Americas, Ottawa, for his assistance in making contacts with shorebird biologists in the Western Hemisphere Shorebird Reserve Network. Also, I would like to thank Pablo Canevari, President, Humedales para las Americas, Argentina; Colleen Hyslop, Latin American Program, Canadian Wildlife Service, Ottawa; and Heidi P. Luquer, Wetlands for the Americas, Manomet Observatory, Massachusetts for their assistance.

I am deeply indebted to Brian Harrington, Manomet Observatory, Massachusetts; Guy Morrison, Canadian Wildlife Service, Ottawa; and George Finney, Director, Canadian Wildlife Service, Atlantic Region, for reading the manuscript and making many useful suggestions. It should be noted, however, that responsibility for any errors in the text is wholly my own.

A special thanks to Dr. Howard Cogswell and Janet Tashjian Hanson, Research Director, San Francisco Bay Bird Observatory for their hospitality. And I would like to express a heartfelt thanks to my manuscript editor, Anne Norman, for her meticulous and insightful suggestions.

The author gratefully acknowledges the assistance of the Canada Council for a Non-Fiction Writing Award, which partially funded research for this book.

Dedicated to
Peter Hicklin and Mary Majka,
whose passion for the science and poetry
of shorebirds
inspired this book

FACING PAGE: *A long-billed curlew uses its namesake bill like a pair of forceps.* DAVID WEINTRAUB

INTRODUCTION

Several years ago, when we moved into our new home, I experienced a confirmation, a rare nod from the natural world, that we had done the right thing. Part of the motivation to move was the closeness to a salt marsh, where I keenly anticipated seeing birds and other wildlife in season. A tidal river flows through our backyard, and across the river is the marsh, a fragment of the great Tantramar marshes that form a landbridge between the Maritime provinces of Nova Scotia and New Brunswick on Canada's Atlantic coast.

That first morning, I was alerted by a familiar, and deeply affecting, sound: *Pita-wee, pita-wee, wee, wee, wee.* I knew without looking what the sound-maker was—a willet. To me, there could be no clearer signal that I was indeed home, for I had had the rare privilege of growing up with the strident cries of willets circumscribing the marsh environment of my childhood. Of all the creatures I had encountered there in the languid, salt-tinged summers, none had moved me more than the willet. Its territorial vocalization simultaneously seemed to proclaim my very own piece of the earth.

Wheeling, I followed the sound, and squinting into the sun, I picked up the silhouette of this swift shorebird planing in for a landing on the marsh. It lit on a hummock and, as willets always do, raised its dark wings to flash the bold white stripes on their undersides. We do not know exactly why willets exhibit this grand gesture, but to me that morning it was the visual equivalent of the shorebird's cry: another "Yes" to the question "Is this home?" Unfortunately for the willet and other shorebirds, our common definition of "home" has engendered not only praise and affection but a growing threat of disenfranchisement.

I grew up at the southwestern tip of Nova Scotia, which for much of the twentieth century was a northern refuge for the eastern subspecies of willet. Once willets had bred up and down the entire Atlantic coast, but their large size, general plumpness, and aggressive behaviour had made them easy targets for hunters. As well, successive generations had diked, drained, and backfilled much of their preferred habitat in the east, the salt marsh.

By the mid-1950s, when I first made my acquaintance with willets, the only place that they bred north of the Carolinas was on the salt marshes of southern Nova Scotia. In summer I saw—and heard!—them daily as they patrolled the marshy bottom of our salt-water farm and scolded me from the tops of black spruce if I ventured too close to their nests secreted under bayberry and wild rose bushes. Their swift flights and piercing calls created in me a lasting love of their kind.

FACING PAGE: *A buff-breasted sandpiper waves to its prospective mate as part of a courtship display on a lek, or dancing ground.* KEVIN T. KARLSON

NEXT PAGE: *A pair of marbled godwits use the upturned bill of the godwit guild to probe for invertebrate prey.* DAVID WEINTRAUB

Part 1

KEEPERS OF THE SHORE

KEEPERS OF THE SHORE

The restlessness of shorebirds, their kinship with the distance and swift seasons, the wistful signal of their voices down the long coastlines of the world make them, for me, the most affecting of wild creatures.

—Peter Matthiessen, *The Wind Birds: Shorebirds of North America*, 1973

For many of us living in North America, our encounters with shorebirds are brief and seasonal, when these swift and restless birds stop over on their epic migrations between northern breeding grounds and far southern wintering areas. For a few weeks, we watch these marbled sky-grey and earth-coloured birds wade in and wing over the wetlands that also attract and nurture us. They become, with us, the keepers of the shorelines, whether it is the shore of an estuary, a prairie slough, or a lake.

This relationship reaches back through time and across gulfs of culture. The agrarian Freemont, who flourished near the shores of Utah's Great Salt Lake between A.D. 700 and 1300, were noted for incising and pecking images onto their pottery. In *Refuge: An Unnatural History of Family and Place*, Terry Tempest Williams contemplates the minimalist markings on a potsherd and suddenly finds them "infinitely familiar." They are long-legged shorebirds standing in the dazzling waters of Great Salt Lake: godwits, curlews, avocets, and stilts—species as well known to modern lake dwellers as to the ancient Freemont.

With the turning of the seasons, our ties to these statuesque birds are renewed. We see them congregated at the water's edge, where they form impressive phalanxes—flocks of tens, hundreds, thousands, or even tens of thousands. Then they are gone, leaving us to wonder about the lives of these fleeting presences.

FACING PAGE: *A flock of shorebirds feeds at Boundary Bay, British Columbia. Shorebirds must consume up to one-third of their body weight every day to meet demands of their energetic lifestyle.* GRAHAM OSBORNE

BIODIVERSITY: LONG LEGS, LONG BILLS, AND SHARP WINGS

To casual observers, shorebirds may appear unremarkable. They are simply those "little brown-and-white birds" along the shore. Few appreciate the dramatic nature of these long-distance travellers. Shorebird migations are among the most spectacular animal movements in the Western Hemisphere, spanning 25 000 kilometres (15,000 miles), much of it over inhospitable oceans. In the case of the red knot and Hudsonian godwit, they travel literally to the ends of the earth, from Canada's high Arctic to Tierra del Fuego, at the tip of South America.

Shorebirds are found on every continent except Antarctica. Numbering 214 species worldwide, they represent a dazzling global biodiversity. About a third of these species touch down in North America on their intercontinental travels, and of these forty-nine species breed here regularly. The shorebirds of North America fall largely into two great families, the plovers (Charadriidae) and the sandpipers (Scolopacidae). Four other families—oystercatchers, jacanas, stilts and avocets, and thick-knees—add only six species to the continental list. These relatively uncommon groups are often striking in their markings, however, which clearly distinguishes them from the blander sandpipers and plovers. The sandpipers—some thirty species strong in North America—are the most diverse group. They include long-legged, slender species, such as the tattlers, dowitchers, godwits, and curlews, and short-legged, stocky species, such as turnstones, phalaropes, woodcock, and snipe. The smallest sandpipers often are called simply "peeps." Sandpipers vary widely in size, however, from the least sandpiper, no bigger than a sparrow, to the largest curlews, the size of small chickens. The plovers, comprising some fifteen species, are a more uniformly compact group—"neckless," with short bodies, large heads, and short bills.

Shorebirds as a group are generally smaller than other unrelated waders—the herons, storks, rails, and cranes—with whom they share wetlands. The eminent Canadian shorebird biologist R.I. Guy Morrison has sorted out the defining characteristics of the shorebird throng: long legs for wading, long bills for probing in muds, and a streamlined body, powered by sharp, dynamic wings. Each of these physical characteristics has evolved to make possible a highly energetic and adaptable lifestyle.

Perhaps the lasting impression of any shorebird encounter is speed. As the nature writer Franklin Russell has observed, "There is no such thing as a slow shorebird." Indeed, I have watched a flock of tens of thousands of semipalmated sandpipers frustrate the fastest of winged predators, the peregrine falcon. To observe a flock of sandpipers streaming through the air is to witness a kind of aerial quicksilver. Their flights are a marvel of aerodynamics. As they bank, the light is absorbed by their dark backs, then reflected by their bright bellies—an illusory show thought to confuse predatory raptors. Sandpipers flow and turn together with such uncanny precision as to make one think they are a single organism.

The most flamboyant of shorebirds, a black-necked stilt shows off its shocking pink legs. DAVID WEINTRAUB

MARINE CREATURES: TUNED TO THE TIDES

Shorebirds belong to the order of birds known as Charadriiformes. Their closest relatives are the gulls, auks, and terns—generally speaking, birds of the ocean and inland waterways. Most shorebirds breed in interior regions along lakes and rivers, or in marshes and meltwater-saturated tundra. As might be expected in a group so richly represented, there are nonconformists to this water-loving lifestyle. The upland sandpiper and mountain plover prefer grassy uplands to the shoreline, whether lapped by salt- or freshwater waves.

For the most part, however, shorebirds are marine creatures. Even for those that nest in the interior, their time on the breeding grounds is short, especially in the Arctic. They spend two-thirds to three-quarters of their year on the migration routes and wintering grounds, largely in tidal environments where they feed on marine invertebrates. By one estimate, 80 per cent of shorebirds are maritime, or coastal, in their lifestyle. Some, like the oystercatchers, are exclusively so, nesting on beaches and salt marshes and feeding on rocky shorelines and tidal flats. Two species of phalaropes—red and red-necked (formerly called northern)—are not only maritime in their habits but positively pelagic, and are sometimes called sea snipes. Red phalaropes spend upwards of three-quarters of their time at sea, more than some marine mammals.

The keen tuning of shorebirds to the tidal nature of the marine environment is patently obvious to anyone who has spent time watching them at their coastal feeding grounds. Each summer, I experience one of the great events in the avian world: the funnelling of up to 2 million migratory shorebirds, 95 per cent of them semipalmated sandpipers, into the upper Bay of Fundy, an ecosystem dominated by its world-famous high tides, of up to 15 metres (50 feet). In the bay, the shorebirds follow the advancing and retreating tide with unflagging alacrity. There is considerable cunning at the root of this strategy as it allows them to snatch the small mudshrimp that become stranded while searching for mates and to probe from the water-softened flats those still hiding in their U-shaped burrows. At low tide, with 5 kilometres (3 miles) of the tidal flats exposed, you could drive by without noticing the shorebird flocks, they are so spread out along the distant tideline. At high tide, however, the incoming tide packs immense concentrations of shorebirds—I have seen up to 200,000 in a single flock—onto a relatively thin cusp of beach.

On their hemispheric migrations, the two maritime species of phalaropes concentrate in areas of tidal upwellings. While on their arctic breeding grounds, these birds employ an ingenious food-gathering strategy. They spin, at the dizzying rate of one revolution per

FACING PAGE: *A flock of sanderlings rests in rockweed. Most shorebirds are marine creatures, spending much of the year in tidal environments.* BARRETT & MACKAY PHOTO

second, creating a whirlpool beneath them that whips up bottom-dwelling larvae. They then harvest the insects with precise pecks of their needle-like beaks. But when they abandon their inland feeding grounds for the coast, they choose areas, such as the Bay of Fundy and California's Monterey Bay, where a natural tidal pump does the food gathering for them, blasting food to the surface. Their wintering grounds, off the coasts of Peru and West Africa, are also tidally turbulent regions, rich in accessible food.

FACING PAGE: *At home on the water, a red-necked, or northern, phalarope catches some shut-eye. Phalaropes, alone among shorebirds, spend long periods at sea.* HÅKAN HJORT/NATURFOTOGRAFERNA

A handsome pair of red phalaropes on their Alaskan nesting grounds. In contrast to the usual pattern in nature, the female (right) is larger than its male partner and mates with more than one male. KEVIN T. KARLSON

FEEDING HABITS: PICKERS AND PROBERS

In her poem "Sandpiper," Elizabeth Bishop observed: "His beak is focussed; he is preoc-cupied,\looking for something, something, something.\Poor bird, he is obsessed!"

Shorebirds consume up to one-third of their body weight every day. They must feed constantly, not only to maintain their daily needs but also to acccumulate the enormous fat reserves required to bridge the often great distances between breeding grounds and wintering areas far to the south. Many demonstrate an uncanny ability to find their inver-tebrate prey. Snipe, for example, are said to sense their earthworm prey through their feet, as if they possessed ground-penetrating radar, and red knots are so successful at locating deeply buried bivalves they, too, are thought to have "a remote sense."

It is possible to distinguish between members of the two major shorebird groups largely by observing their feeding habits. Dennis Paulson, in his comprehensive book *Shorebirds of the Pacific Northwest*, labels all shorebirds as either "pickers" or "probers." Plovers—the pickers—have large eyes and feed by sight: they run between prey, stop, and peck, the so-called peck-and-run method. Sandpipers, with their small eyes, are probers; they use their longer, sensory-tipped bills to search for food and can often be seen dili-gently mining an invertebrate burrow with a characteristic sewing-machine motion.

The sanderling, the palest of the sandpiper group, is familiar to any North American who has spent time on a beach watching waves lap ashore. I have watched sanderlings skitter along the tideline. Their stiff-legged gait makes them look "like clockwork toys," to borrow the metaphor of Les Line, *Audubon*'s longtime editor. Their head movements are mechanical, their probes so abrupt and shallow that the term "stitches" is used to describe them. They seem, in fact, to be stitching the frilly lace of the waves to the conti-nent's hemline.

Of course, nothing is ever simple in the natural world. Some sandpipers do not prefer soft, sandy shorelines at all. A sandpiper that prefers the rocky coast is the well-named ruddy turnstone. Having both an unmistakable appearance and a distinctive behaviour, this brightly marked bird offers a reprieve to the shorebird watcher's tricky task of identifying confusingly drab sandpipers. Black markings on the head and a passionately chestnut back, as well as carrot-orange legs, single it out from any other candidates among the shorebird crowd. The second half of its name comes from its curious habit of searching for food by overturning clumps of seaweed or small stones, whereupon it chases its rudely exposed prey in a plover-like manner. Other "rock-haunting" sandpipers are the purple sandpiper, which winters as far north as Newfoundland, and its Pacific counterpart, the rock sandpiper.

FACING PAGE: *Plovers are expert pickers, but this black-bellied plover has its work cut out for it in a tug-of-war with a marine worm.* TOM VEZO

Despite these notable exceptions, most sandpipers exploit the muddy environments of marsh, mud flat, and tundra. To do so, they have evolved an arsenal of specialized bills. The sandpiper bill is not the rigid, insensitive instrument it might seem. The tip is mobile, and under the horny cover of the beak is a concentration of tactile organs used to sense prey. The tip has some of the attributes of a finger, in fact, as the upper mandible is controlled by muscles and can grasp worms or larvae and move them along the length of the bill to allow for swallowing.

Dowitchers, snipe, and woodcock all have long, relatively straight bills; godwits have long, slightly upturned bills. Curlew bills are not only extravagantly long but curved dramatically downward to allow them to pursue prey secreted deep in convoluted burrows. The most exaggerated example belongs to the largest of the North American shorebirds, the long-billed curlew.

I saw my first long-billed curlew on its wintering grounds in San Francisco Bay, California. Its size was arresting, even beside statuesque willets. Its cinnamon colouring also made it stand out beside the drab grey of the western willets in winter. But it was the beak, a preposterously long instrument—they grow to up to 20 centimetres (8 inches)—downcurved at the tip like a pair of surgical forceps, that riveted my attention. I watched as the curlew inserted its fabled bill slowly and deliberately into the mud flats, to its full length, and then retracted it, dangling a saltwater worm nearly as long as the bill itself.

Not surprisingly, this prodigious bill can serve as either picker or probe. Naturalist C. W. Wickersham described the catholic tastes of the long-billed curlew in *The Auk* in 1902:

> Crawfish, small crabs, snails, periwinkles, toads, worms, larvae, grasshoppers, crickets, beetles, caterpillars when found on the ground, spiders, flies, butterflies and berries, especially dewberries, all play minor or major parts in their diet. The worms, larvae, etc. are pulled out of the ground by the long bill, the end of which may act as a finger having separate muscles to control it, and often it is sunk into the ground as far as it will go to reach some unwilling victim. The crustaceans are taken on the beach, or, discovered beneath the surface by the probing bill, are pulled out and eaten. The berries are neatly picked off the bushes, while butterflies and other insects are taken on the wing.

Bill shape acts as a means of sorting out feeding niches among shorebirds. Ornithologists call this "resource partitioning." Where a shorebird is likely to be found in relation to the tideline and other birds is determined by the length of its bill and, to a degree, the length of its legs.

I witnessed this in San Francisco Bay National Wildlife Refuge. The tide was receding, exposing a swath of mud flat that curved under the Dumbarton Bridge. In the strong

FACING PAGE: *A greater yellowlegs has a reflective moment in its marshland habitat. Notorious for their strident voices, greater yellowlegs were known as telltales by early North American settlers.*
ROBERT LANKINEN/FIRST LIGHT

morning light, I could see hundreds of small shorebirds, in ranks, spread out northward along the freshly exposed shoreline.

Because of their position closest to shore, my guide, Dr. Howard Cogswell, author of *Water Birds of California,* confirmed that these were western sandpipers, without even having to look at them. To the south, Cogswell pointed out, the darker and slightly larger dunlins were mixed in with the western sandpipers.

Farther from shore, in deeper wading territory, were the larger shorebirds with their longer legs and bills. Closest to the tideline was a small flock of marbled godwits, lovely in their cinnamon plummage and sporting the long, slightly upturned bill of the godwit guild. Also spread out along the tideline, clustered in more or less discrete groups, were the drably attired willets as well as the plump-looking long-billed dowitchers. All the birds were busily feeding.

Cogswell pointed out that there were basically three types of food available in San Francisco Bay: the small clam *Macoma,* polychaete worms, and amphipod crustaceans. Western sandpipers were feeding on the latter, because their bills can accommodate only the smallest prey. As pick feeders, the willets were plucking clams near the surface, while the godwits inserted the full length of their bills, probing for more deeply burrowing invertebrates like the worms.

To observe the shorebird with the most diverse feeding repertoire, the American avocet, we backtracked to the upper reaches of the bay. Almost all of the shore marshlands had been converted to salt evaporation ponds in the last century. Here we found flocks of both members of the Recurvirostridae family—avocets and stilts. These are arguably the most elegant of the shorebird clans, with their striking markings, long, sculptural body lines, and spindly legs. I saw the black-necked stilts first, wading in the pond on their extraordinarily long and delicate legs, which are a shocking pink. Between graceful strides, the stilts were pecking at tiny animals, no doubt brine shrimp in these, the saltiest of the evaporation ponds. The long legs of the stilts and avocets allow them to forage in areas inaccessible to many of the smaller sandpipers; in addition, avocets, like the phalaropes, frequently swim and even tip up to feed like marsh ducks.

The avocets were roosting on the tiny islands in the salt pond. They had exchanged the almost pink breast colour of breeding season for the more formal bluish-grey of winter. (Their similarly coloured legs earn them the sobriquet "bluestockings.") Their size, the clear demarcation of monochrome colouring, and, especially, the rakishly upturned bill delighted my eye. It is the recurved bill that gives avocets a feeding advantage. They can pick or probe with it, but they can also "scythe." When scything, they run rapidly through the water sweeping their scimitar-shaped bill back and forth in the water column or underlying soupy mud, at the same time stirring up and snagging their prey.

Yellowlegs also practise this scything technique, sometimes with comic results. All fall, the yellowlegs feed in the tidepools of the marsh behind my home, lingering until the marsh ices over in November. Once I watched as three stalked through a tidepool in concert, like a predatory corps de ballet. They were submerged to their brilliant white bellies, which were reflected, tutu-like, on the tidepool surface. They strutted hither and thither, zigzagging through the pool in a random, seeming-mad dash. As they ran they plunged their heads into the water and scythed, supposedly in an attempt to mow down their elusive silver prey, minnows—to no effect, as far as I could see on this occasion.

Perhaps the most specialized feeders of the North American shorebirds are the oystercatchers. These are strictly coastal birds. Two species occur: a pied variety, the American oystercatcher, on the coastlines of the mid-Atlantic states, Gulf of Mexico, and Baja California; and a monochrome variety, the black oystercatcher, which is strictly a sedentary denizen of the Pacific coast of North America. The yellow eyes with red eye ring and the red bill make these large shorebirds impossible to confuse with any other. Their most interesting feature, however, is their triangular bill—a clever evolutionary cross between knife and chisel for the daunting task of opening oysters and other bivalves.

Oystercatchers have adopted two ingenious strategies in overcoming their prey. They either plunge their bills into the open shell of an unwary mollusk, instantly severing the muscles holding the two halves of the shell together, or they smash the shell with a few well-directed blows. What makes these techniques more remarkable is that they are learned. Parents feed the young for up to a year, passing on their acumen as either "stabbers" or "hammerers."

BREEDING GROUNDS AND SKY DANCING

Shorebirds are gregarious. On their migratory stopover sites and wintering grounds, they congregate in flocks varying in size from a few individuals to hundreds of thousands. During the breeding season, however, they disperse.

Few of us have had an opportunity to observe their breeding behaviour, because shorebirds prefer northern, largely unpopulated regions. Most species favour breeding habitats with low vegetation. Such extensive untreed habitat is primarily found in the arctic tundra and tundra–boreal forest. Forty-one species breed in these areas north of 60 degrees. The tundra and muskeg, besides providing open space, also produce vast quantities of larval and adult insects, which fuel the high-energy demands of the egg-laying and brooding periods. Sandpipers tend to predominate in the vast, undisturbed, northern breeding grounds.

Other treeless habitat occurs along North America's eastern and western coasts, where seven species breed, including the oystercatchers and Wilson's plover. Of greater extent and importance are the Great Plains, breeding grounds for a dozen species of shorebirds. Here, extensive grasslands harbour their own typical species: in the drier west of the short-grass prairie, the long-billed curlew and mountain plover; farther to the east, where greater humidity produces tall-grass prairie, the marbled godwit, willet, and upland sandpiper.

A few of the temperate breeders are well known to most North Americans. Perhaps the most familiar is the common snipe, which breeds across all of temperate North America and Eurasia. From my earliest days on the farm, I remember my sense of exhilaration at hearing the winnowing of the common snipe, as it performed its ecstatic nuptial flight above the sodden pastures. It was one of the welcome accompaniments of spring. The sound, phonetically rendered as *huhuhuhuhuhuhuhuhu*, has been variously described as a bleating, drumming, and winnowing.

But what causes this "spirit-suggesting sound," as Henry David Thoreau called it?

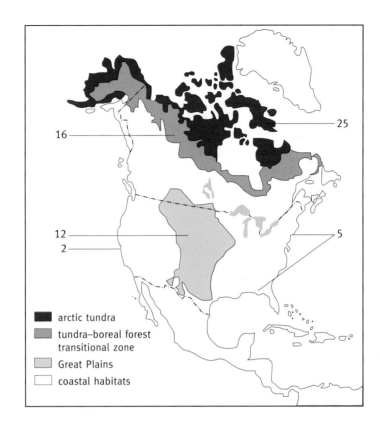

arctic tundra

tundra–boreal forest transitional zone

Great Plains

coastal habitats

The number of species of shorebirds that breed in major unforested or partially forested biomes in North America is shown. These include the Great Plains and the Atlantic and Pacific coasts, although most species prefer the far northern tundra and muskeg as breeding grounds.

Source: Marshall Howe, "Breeding Ecology of North American Shorebirds: Patterns and Constraints," Fig. 2, in Hugh Boyd, ed., First Western Hemisphere Waterfowl and Waterbird Symposium.

The winnowing sound made by the common snipe has earned this shore-bird an uncommon number of folk-names: "horse gawk" in the Orkneys, "heaven's goat" in Lithuania, and "sheep of the marshes" in Wales. In Alaska, the Nunamiut call the snipe "weather maker." JAN TÖVE/ NATURFOTOGRAFERNA

Ruffs, a Eurasian species, perform an elaborate courtship display on their dancing ground, or lek. Males alone sport these impressive collars in breeding season, a striking example of polymorphism. JAN VAN DE KAM

When I hear winnowing, instinctively I look up, and there, silhouetted against the sky, is the circling snipe. Snipe circle 30 to 60 metres (100 to 200 feet) above their territory, then dive headlong at a 45 degree angle. As they dive, they fan out their tail feathers at right angles to the body, causing them to vibrate in the onrushing air. The movement of the wings, superimposed on the tail-feather vibrations, creates the characteristic quavering sound. Males perform this aerial trick as part of a territorial display when they first arrive on the breeding grounds, and then more frequently after the females arrive, when it also plays a part in pair formation.

The American woodcock—the "hermit of the alders"—also produces wing-twittering noises to attract a mate. Writer-wildlife biologist Aldo Leopold described "the sky dance" of the woodcock over his native Wisconsin in *A Sand County Almanac:*

> The bird flutters skyward in a series of wide spirals, emitting a musical twitter. Up and up he goes, the spirals steeper and smaller, the twittering louder and louder, until the performer is only a speck in the sky. Then, without warning, he tumbles like a crippled plane, giving voice in a soft liquid warble that a March bluebird might envy.

In the shorebird world, the most elaborate mating ritual belongs to a Eurasian species, the ruff. Although ruffs breed across the northern extent of Eurasia and winter in southern Africa, they annually appear as wind-blown vagrants both on the Atlantic coast and in Alaska, where the first North American breeding for this species was recorded in 1976. A large, portly sandpiper, the ruff is relatively nondescript—as its tribe is wont to be—for most of the year. But at breeding season the male undergoes a remarkable transformation. The most spectacular of its accoutrements is the large collar that flares around the neck like an avian equivalent of the frilly muslin ruffs common to the courts of Elizabeth I, or, to invoke a modern analogy, the cape once donned by the king of rock and roll. These impressive plumes run the gamut of colours from rufous to purplish-black, brown to yellow, black to white, and can be solid, speckled, or spotted. On top of the head are two flared tufts, and the face itself is covered in colourful wattles. The female, called a reeve, undergoes no such transformation. This is the only species of shorebird in which the male and female bear different names, and their physical differences during the breeding season probably constitute the most striking example of polymorphism (having several different forms) in the avian world. Not only does the ruff undergo a complete makeover to attract a mate, it performs a ritualistic territorial display—a dance. The dancing ground is called a lek, and the male returns to the same one year after year. Peter Matthiessen, in *The Wind Birds*, describes this display: "[He] struts, twirls and postures on his mound or stamping area and fights with others of his gorgeous sex by leaping high into the air or seizing another's ruff in antic jealousy." So impressed with the ruff's histri-

onics were the Chukchi aboriginals of Siberia, they paid homage to this behaviour in an imitative dance.

The ruff's lek displays are actually a form of ritualized aggression. There are two groups of males on the lek: independent males and satellite males. The independent males are generally darker and occupy the central portion of the lek. They defend their territory vigorously. The more central males consequently mate with the most females—the object of the exercise.

The buff-breasted sandpiper, a small sandpiper that regularly breeds in the Canadian and Alaskan high Arctic, also displays on leks. The males defend larger territories than ruffs, 10 to 50 metres (30 to 160 feet), giving chase to other males, and wing-flashing and wing-waving to repel competitors and attract mates. They also "flutter-jump," sometimes in unison with another male, the two rising 6 to 12 metres (20 to 40 feet) into the air.

FACING PAGE: *A denizen of rocky coasts, the ruddy turnstone cannot be mistaken for any other shorebird, with its chestnut markings and carrot-orange legs.* KLAS RUNE/ NATURFOTOGRAFERNA

MATING SYSTEMS

Shorebirds display a greater diversity of mating systems—monogamy, polygyny, and polyandry—than any other group of birds. Ecological factors, in particular food supply and risk from predators, determine which approach is adopted.

Most shorebirds are monogamous, as cooperation in the harsh northern breeding grounds seems to pay genetic dividends. The monogamous lifestyle of the dunlin, for example, protects against predation of the nests and cuts down on egg chilling, which can delay hatching time and reduce the chick's overall chances of survival. Surfbird and western, purple, semipalmated, least, Baird's, rock, and stilt sandpipers share this monogamous, territorial social system. Shorebirds, however, rarely form lifelong pair bonds, with the possible exception of the oystercatchers, which may mate for life.

Other sandpipers have adopted promiscuous mating strategies. White-rumped and sharp-tailed sandpipers are polygynous, that is, one male mates with more than one female, while each female mates with only one male, which takes no part in incubation. Although this is the rule in the animal kingdom, it is relatively rare among birds, where it appears the two-parent system common to monogamy better ensures survival of the young—and therefore a better chance for both mates to perpetuate their DNA. Why then do some species choose polygyny? Again, it seems to relate to the best use of available resources. If males defend territories with widely differing resource bases, then it is advantageous for the female to become the second mate of the superior male rather than to settle, monogamously, for a male that holds an inferior territory. The male also derives a benefit: by associating with more than one female, it increases its chances of passing on its genetic material.

Perhaps the most ingenious breeding strategy in birds is polyandry, literally "many males." Fewer than 1 per cent of bird species practise polyandry; interestingly, most are shorebirds. Reversing the usual roles in the animal kingdom, the female mates with more than one male. Often the male then undertakes all or most of the parental duties, and the female assumes the aggressive role of defending territories of her male consorts. In the case of phalaropes, the female is the larger and more colourful of the pair, in contrast to the usual pattern of male showiness.

Polyandry is also practised by the spotted sandpiper, or "spotty," as it is affectionately known to birders. It breeds throughout temperate North America and therefore is among the most familiar and easily recognized of our shorebirds. In the breeding season, its breast is prominently flecked with the spots that give the small sandpiper its name. It also

FACING PAGE: *A pair of American avocets perform a post-copulatory display, crossing bills, as the male drapes his wing over the female.* ARTHUR MORRIS/BIRDS AS ART

has two readily apparent behavioural ticks. When standing, it teeters obsessively, its tail bobbing up and down. When it takes flight—usually short-haul hops—only its wingtips "flutter." Almost any lakeshore and streamside will have its resident spotties: they teeter, then flutter a few yards away at your approach—teeter and flutter, ad infinitum.

Perhaps because of its familiarity and its innocuous habits, we little suspect what an interesting sex life the spotty has. Why the spotty employs polyandry may relate to its having adopted the temperate regions as its breeding grounds. The short arctic and sub-arctic breeding season prevents most shorebirds from raising more than one brood. The longer breeding season in the temperate regions makes it possible through the efficiency of polyandry. Although the female spotty might manage to lay five complete clutches in the six- to seven-week breeding season, each clutch requires three weeks of incubation. Polyandry provides the solution, as the males incubate the eggs while the female seeks another mate. Nevertheless, most spotted sandpiper females are successful in raising only two clutches per year, because of an acute shortage of males. Once males start incubation, they are no longer available as prospective mates.

A variation on this system—called sequential polyandry—is used by the mountain plover and the sanderling. Each female lays a clutch of eggs that is incubated by the males, followed by a second clutch that she incubates herself.

FACING PAGE: *A spotted sandpiper checks on its egg clutch. Through a mating system called polyandry, literally "many males," the female spotty is able to raise more than one clutch of eggs per year.* MARK K. PECK/VALAN PHOTOS

Precocial killdeer chicks nestle among violets, heralding another spring in Montana. ART WOLFE

THE SHOREBIRD YEAR: FAST FORWARD

A few years ago, on April 7, alerted by the familiar call *killdee, killdee,* I looked out on my narrow strip of lawn, still half-covered in snow, to see a killdeer. This is the most wide-spread and best-known shorebird in North America. The two prominent black bands on its breast, the rufous tail feathers, and the distinctive call are giveaways for this large, handsome plover. Neither is the killdeer shy. Little perturbed by human presence, it often prefers to nest in farm fields, on suburban lawns, and even on asphalt roofs.

The killdeer was foraging in its robin-like manner, skittering from one bare patch of ground to another. The day before, I had seen my first two robins, the traditional harbinger of spring. Curiously, killdeer and robin—one rufous-tailed, the other red-breasted—are often the first birds to move north into their breeding grounds.

Later I surprised a pair of killdeer. They fanned out their gorgeous rufous tails and spread wide their wings to advertise this was their home turf. In the weeks to follow, I would often hear the male loudly proclaiming its territory.

It was an insistent reminder that, all along the Atlantic seaboard, other shorebirds were heading north from the Neotropics, with more than half a million pouring into Delaware Bay alone. Simultaneously, an avalanche of shorebirds was passing along the west coast of North America in March, April, and May, stopping off in San Francisco Bay, California; Grays Harbor, Washington; and Boundary Bay, British Columbia. And through the Great Plains, the greatest conduit for migratory shorebirds in spring, great flocks were funnelling north to their birthplace, to begin again the turning of the shorebird's year.

The northern summer is short. Much must be accomplished on the breeding grounds. A succession of critical functions must be performed for successful rearing of young—territory establishment, courtship, nest building, laying, and incubation, care, and fledging of young—before weather begins to deteriorate and the birds of summer again must turn southward.

Because of this short time frame, the shorebird clock seems to be set to fast forward. The incubation period for most shorebirds is relatively brief; for example, for the semi-palmated sandpiper it is an average of twenty days. Shorebird chicks are extremely precocial, that is, they are capable of moving around on their own very soon after hatching. Semipalmated sandpiper chicks are born with their eyes open and legs large enough to carry them forward into the world within hours. As soon as they dry, they stumble from the nest cup and begin pecking for insects. On day one, the chicks preen, exercise their wings, and crouch when warned by parents. The parents do not feed the young but will lead them to foraging areas. They also brood them for warmth during the first week, and guard them constantly for their first two weeks of life.

While on the breeding grounds, the diminutive shorebirds must rely on a grab-bag of distraction displays to defend their young. Many employ the common gambit of broken wing displays, the killdeer being a past master of this oldest trick in the book. A rather more innovative means of decoying a predator is the so-called rodent run practised by a number of arctic-breeding shorebirds, including the dunlin, pectoral sandpiper, and sanderling. On being approached by a predator, the shorebird runs off with a high piping call, which sounds like a rodent squeaking. The bird tilts its head forward and fluffs up its feathers to resemble fur. What makes the ruse more convincing is the shorebird's posture: it drags both wings, simulating a second pair of legs, and runs in a zigzag manner, in imitation of a fleeing rodent. The overall effect may be heightened by the dark median stripe on the upper tail of species such as the purple sandpiper—markings that mimic the back pattern of collared lemmings. This seems to be a distraction display targeted at predators like the arctic fox, which is foxy enough—or thinks it is—to know that it would rather pursue an earthbound rodent than an adult shorebird capable of flight.

Shorebird voices are well suited to open spaces. The loud, low-frequency sounds carry well across the tundra and other treeless breeding grounds, serving to declare territory, attract mates, and signal danger. Also, many shorebirds show a flash of white under their tail in flight. Like the warning flag of the white-tailed deer, the purpose is probably to raise alarm at the unwelcome approach of predators. The wing flash of the willet and the rufous rump of the killdeer also are considered "threat colours," deployed to startle a potential predator. Certainly, their shrill and well-exercised voices serve to discourage interlopers.

Shorebird chicks, however, are soon independent. Female semipalmated sandpipers desert the brood within ten days after they hatch, leaving the male to care for the young. It is thought that the female, suffering from the high-energy demand of egg production, must leave in order to increase her own chances of survival. She heads south to be first on the energy-rich feeding grounds along the migratory route. The male deserts the brood at about the time the chicks fledge, usually two weeks after hatching. Finally, the juveniles themselves leave the breeding grounds to embark on their immense journey, setting in motion a new cycle of the shorebird year.

ABOVE: *A lesser golden plover performs a distraction display on its northern breeding grounds, where the arctic fox is a major predator.* ALBERT KUHNIGK/VALAN PHOTOS

FACING PAGE: *A killdeer strikes a familiar pose, feigning injury. The rufous rump also may function as a "threat colour," designed to startle predators.* WAYNE LANKINEN

PAGE 38: *A flock of red knots trails over a mountain peak. One of the most impressive of long-distance migrants, knots are circumpolar breeders that migrate to all continents.* HANNU HAUTALA

Part 2

HEMISPHERIC TRAVELLERS

HEMISPHERIC TRAVELLERS

On cool August nights you can hear their whistled signals as they
[upland sandpipers] set wing for the pampas, to prove again the
age-old unity of the Americas. Hemisphere solidarity is new among
statesmen, but not among the feathered navies of the sky.

—Aldo Leopold, *A Sand County Almanac,* 1949

Several years ago, I witnessed the spectacle of shorebird migration from a bird's-eye view, when I flew the coastline of James and Hudson Bays—the northern, inland seas that funnel into the heart of North America.

The shadow of the Twin Otter, like that of a giant raptor, menaced over the emerald ribbon of marsh bordering the bay, stirring flurries of shorebirds from their feeding grounds. Hour after hour, the subarctic taiga of the Hudson Bay Lowlands unfolded below us—an intricate fabric of verdancy, splashed with arabesques of yellow ragwort and the sinuous lines of muddy creeks as pleasing as the patterns of a Persian rug. At Cape Henrietta Maria, where James Bay opens to Hudson Bay, pack ice greeted us, though it was only August 1. The shorebirds could take a hint: in this latitude, summer was over, and it was time to point the arrow of migration south.

We moved north against this southerly flux. Although we were airborne for ten hours, never once were we out of sight of a marvellous diversity and abundance of birds: tens and hundreds of Hudsonian godwits and their cinnamon-coloured cousins, marbled godwits, along with whimbrels, yellowlegs, dowitchers, and knots—and thousands of peeps. Winged clouds.

"It's an incredible coast when everything is on the go," Guy Morrison told me before we took off from Moosonee, Ontario, at the south end of James Bay. "The coastline func-

tions very much like a migratory highway. You have this ribbon leading for 1000 kilometres [600 miles] along the coast of Hudson Bay and James Bay, into which is packed these enormous populations of geese, ducks, and shorebirds, working their way south—so there's very much a concentration or funnelling effect as the birds move southward."

It was here, in 1974, that Morrison discovered a flock of 10,000 Hudsonian godwits. They would fly directly from James Bay to the north coast of South America—4500 kilometres (2800 miles)—the longest nonstop migration performed by any shorebird. As well, to his astonishment, he counted 15,000 red knots, establishing this area as one of international importance for this species.

"In many ways, the whole coastline is an unappreciated jewel of the Canadian landscape," he told me. To the ornithologist it is a jewel—a place both beautiful and bountiful. For birds it is a vital staging area, a place to pause and fatten up for the long journey ahead.

For two days, I was compelled to see the world as a migrating bird might. Skimming a few hundred metres above the marsh "highway," I noted the tracks of caribou, themselves migrants, working in serpentine fashion across the intertidal zone; the white bulks of polar bears who had come ashore on ice floes to pass the short subarctic summer wallowing in the mud flats and marsh pools in an effort to combat the plague of flies and surprising heat; and pods of belugas, mothers with their newborns, rubbing and milling at the mouths of estuaries to which they migrate every year. As I moved through the birds' aerial world, my questions about the mystery of migration grew with each passing hour.

WHY SHOREBIRDS MIGRATE:
MARATHONERS OF THE BIRD WORLD

The overriding question is, Why migrate at all? Perhaps it is the wrong question. The chief evolutionary weapon that birds possess is their wings. Ecologically, birds and migration are inseparable: it is, except in rare instances, the very foundation of their existence.

"There's nothing strange in birds migrating," observes Theunis Piersma, a Dutch shorebird biologist. "Almost all over the world resources change in the course of the seasons, so if you can fly the most logical thing to do is to track the resources, to track the absence of predators, and to track the availability of breeding sites: that's why they have wings. I think a better question is, Why do some birds not migrate?"

Shorebirds, as a group, are the marathoners of the avian world. They stitch together an existence with the long thread of migration, which joins two, or more, ecological niches—in the case of shorebirds, a tapestry of wetlands. These green, shimmering places are separated by vast distances, spread out over the length and breadth of two continents. Each of these water-enriched habitats satisfies a different physiological need. Shorebirds need energy for breeding foremost, and then for replacing their feathers (the annual moult), as well as for daily living (subsistence). The far-flung network of coastal and interior wetlands, rich in invertebrates, is critical to their ability to complete their annual cycle. Wetlands are links in a migratory chain vital to the very survival of whole shorebird populations.

Fundamental to the phenomenon of migration is energy: each bird must balance its budget of energy intake and expenditures. The highest energy demands are in the breeding season, especially for production of the eggs. Studies have shown that breeding birds sustain metabolic rates equivalent to Tour de France bicyclists or arctic explorers. Since productivity is seasonal, even in the tropics, birds migrate to maximize their intake. In the south, food supply is sufficient for subsistence but not for breeding. Shorebirds go north (where they comprise the most significant arctic birdlife) to take advantage of the explosion of food resources fuelled by the long hours of sunlight. Also, the melting of the tundra creates a landscape of shallow lakes floating atop the permafrost—perfect habitat for wading shorebirds.

There are other advantages in the northern regions. There are relatively few nest-raiding predators, a vital factor for birds that nest on the ground in open, treeless terrain. Studies have also shown that most predation of shorebirds takes place at night, which, in summer, is short to nonexistent in the land of the midnight sun. There is yet another reason for breeding in the Northern Hemisphere, which can be visualized if you ask yourself

FACING PAGE: *A lesser golden plover settles on a perfectly camouflaged nest in the Arctic tundra. Most shorebirds breed in the north, a vast territory with rich food resources and few nest-raiding predators.* FRED BRUEMMER

PAGES 46–47: *Rare visitors to the California coast, bar-tailed godwits occasionally are blown off course in their migration from breeding grounds in Alaska to wintering areas in the Pacific islands and New Zealand.* ART WOLFE

why shorebirds do not breed in the far south of South America, which also has a summer and winter. If you imagine the tapering tail of Tierra del Fuego and Patagonia inverted and superimposed on the vast arctic lands of North America, the answer becomes obvious: there is just not enough breeding territory in the south.

The underlying assumption about bird migration is that populations migrate if it ensures that their survival rate is greater than if they remained on the breeding ground. For high arctic breeders, staying put is not an option—they must move. There are trade-offs, however, as migration itself is costly. Studies conducted in Suriname suggest that migration may account for half of the total natural mortality. But if short-distance migrants reduce the risk of mortality due to the rigours of migration, the long-distance migrants take that risk in order to reach richer feeding grounds and therefore reap the benefits of better conditioning. Studies of two subspecies of knots in Europe indicate that the population that breeds in Siberia and winters in the more congenial climate of West Africa has a 10 per cent higher annual survival rate than the population that breeds in Canada and Greenland and winters in northern Europe, despite the demands of a longer migration.

FACING PAGE: *A ruddy turnstone rests on an iceberg in Canada's eastern Arctic. These shorebirds breed in North America and winter in Europe, using Iceland as a migratory stepping stone.* JAN VAN DE KAM

THE MIGRATORY CHALLENGE: A LONG LEAP

Not all shorebirds are long-distance migrants: oystercatchers are nonmigratory, woodcock migrate only short distances, and avocets, stilts, and dunlins migrate moderate distances, wintering, for the most part, in the southern United States. Of the forty-nine shorebird species that breed in North America, however, forty migrate to wintering sites in the temperate and tropical regions in Central and South America; thirty-one species fly annually between the Arctic and South America, with most birds making a round trip of 12 000 kilometres (7500 miles), and some, like the red knot, traversing 25 000 kilometres (15,000 miles) annually. It is a curious characteristic of shorebirds' migration that those that breed farthest north also winter farthest south—a phenomenon dubbed "leap-frogging."

Shorebirds whose breeding and nonbreeding grounds are widely separated must replenish their fat reserves, accumulating and burning several times their body weight, in order to complete their journey. They do so by exploiting a chain of staging areas. Often, however, they take giant leaps of 4000 kilometres (2500 miles) at a time.

Before birds begin migrating, they undergo hormonal changes, inducing them to lay down fat, and only when they have accumulated sufficient reserves do they begin their journey. Shorebirds that make migrations of 3000 to 4000 kilometres (1800 to 2500 miles) over inhospitable ecological barriers, such as oceans, glaciers, and deserts, first must double their body weight. This reserve of fat will carry them to their landfall, in a nonstop flight of three to four days. This is equivalent to a human running continuous four-minute miles for sixty hours—a feat beyond the realm of human comprehension. As Fred Bodsworth has written of the Eskimo curlew's pectorals: "[They are] gram for gram among the strongest of animal tissue on earth."

Birds do not merely rely on the raw storage of energy to make these epic voyages. They take advantage of climatic conditions, in particular tail winds, to succesfully complete their journey. Birds are amazingly sensitive barometers able to anticipate the passage of cold fronts, which supply an extra push and thereby help preserve energy.

Radar studies have shown that shorebirds staging from northeast North America first wait for the passage of a northwesterly wind. This sets them on a southeasterly course. If this flight line were extrapolated, most would wind up in West Africa. The birds, in fact, do maintain a steady compass course. However, in the area of the Sargasso Sea, they encounter northeasterly trade winds that steadily push them back towards their destination, the north coast of South America. Taking advantage of these same winds, Columbus and his crew first recorded the large flights of migrating birds.

FACING PAGE: *The well-named wandering tattler stretches a pinion. A northern breeder, it migrates along the Pacific coasts of North and South America, and across the Pacific Ocean to New Guinea.*
ADRIAN DORST

With wind assistance, shorebirds are able to maintain average speeds of 75 kilometres (45 miles) per hour. The normal flight time is sixty to seventy hours, plus or minus twelve hours. Most arrive at their South American landfall with some fat reserves in store. Juveniles, however, making this journey for the first time, may not only exhaust all of their fat but draw upon muscle protein as well in completing this gruelling ocean crossing.

En route to their wintering grounds, shorebirds fly at a mean height of 2000 metres (6500 feet) but some flocks reach altitudes of 6000 metres (20,000 feet). Baird's sandpipers follow the Rocky and Andes mountain chains on their migratory path and therefore must fly at 4000 metres (13,000 feet) or higher, and Eurasian curlews and godwits regularly cross the Himalayas' highest peaks. There may be aerodynamic advantages to such high flying. Air density decreases at greater heights, which means the migrating birds encounter less resistance. But resulting gains in speed and decreases in energy consumption would be modest. More likely, the birds seek altitudes where they can optimize tail winds and minimize head winds. In rainy or foggy weather, however, shorebirds often dip down below the weather ceiling, skimming just above the sea's surface.

FACING PAGE: *Dunlins glean the invertebrate riches of a mud flat near Blaine, Washington. Migrants often fully exploit the food resources of such migratory staging areas.*
R. HAMAGUCHI/TONY STONE IMAGES

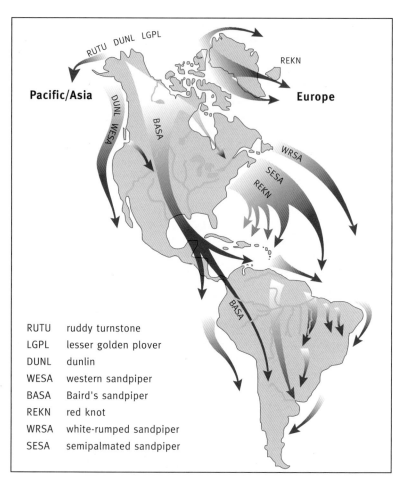

Pacific/Asia

Europe

RUTU   ruddy turnstone
LGPL   lesser golden plover
DUNL   dunlin
WESA   western sandpiper
BASA   Baird's sandpiper
REKN   red knot
WRSA   white-rumped sandpiper
SESA   semipalmated sandpiper

Shorebirds breeding in North America follow three major pathways on their autumn migration. Some fly westward to Asia, others eastward to Europe, but the majority fly south, to the southern United States and Mexico and to Central and South America. Some species take a different route on their northbound and southbound journeys.

Source: R.I.G. Morrison, "Migration Systems of Some New World Shorebirds," Fig. 1, in J. Burger and B.L. Olla, eds., Behavior of Marine Animals. *Vol. 6,* Shorebirds: Migration and Foraging Behavior.

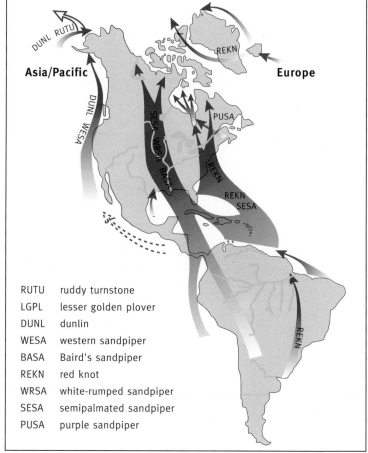

Asia/Pacific

Europe

RUTU   ruddy turnstone
LGPL   lesser golden plover
DUNL   dunlin
WESA   western sandpiper
BASA   Baird's sandpiper
REKN   red knot
WRSA   white-rumped sandpiper
SESA   semipalmated sandpiper
PUSA   purple sandpiper

MIGRATION CORRIDORS: SKY RIVERS

The migration patterns of most far northern, North American shorebirds fall into three general categories. First, there are those breeding in the northeastern Canadian high Arctic and wintering in Europe. These include a red knot subspecies that breeds on Ellesmere Island, with the ruddy turnstone, sanderling, and ringed plover probably following a similar route. Purple sandpipers that breed on Baffin Island may also migrate to Europe via Iceland. Second, there are those breeding across the central North American Arctic and wintering in North, Central, and South America, forming the majority of species. Third, some species breed in northern Alaska and migrate to wintering areas in Asia and the Pacific, including whimbrel and wandering tattler. The bristle-thighed curlew migrates to remote Pacific islands—a feat that requires pinpoint navigational accuracy and endurance.

Unlike perching birds (passerines), which migrate on broad fronts, shorebirds tend to stream into relatively narrow corridors—rivers in the sky. Major migratory corridors within North America follow the Pacific and Atlantic coasts, with a third route through the Gulf of Mexico and the Great Plains. Each species has evolved a variation on this general pattern. In autumn white-rumped sandpipers, for example, use the most northeasterly parts of the Atlantic seaboard of Canada and the United States, being especially abundant in Labrador and the Gulf of St. Lawrence. For this reason they are relatively less common in Maritime Canada and New England. They then make a direct flight across the North Atlantic to the north coast of South America. After replenishing their reserves, they overfly Amazonia to wintering grounds in southern Brazil and Uruguay, some reaching as far south as Tierra del Fuego. Lesser golden plover, and Eskimo curlew—what few remain— also follow this route.

Some species take a different route on their southbound and northbound journeys, however, with the autumn migration usually being east of the spring corridor. Thus their migratory path descibes a transhemispheric ellipse. Semipalmated sandpipers that use the Atlantic seaboard flyway in the autumn, for instance, in spring prefer instead to fly north through the centre of the continent, taking advantage of major interior wetlands, such as Cheyenne Bottoms in Kansas and the Quill Lakes in Saskatchewan. As well, they hopscotch through prairie pothole country, gleaning, getting fat. The most obvious explanation for this seasonal shift is availability of food. In the autumn, more than a million semipalmated sandpipers stage in the Bay of Fundy, whereas they are a rarity in spring. This probably relates to the late ice cover in Maritime Canada, which retards the production of invertebrates. Delaware Bay, on the other hand, is a major spring staging area, owing to the prolific production of horseshoe crab eggs there in late May.

Sanderlings string out along the west coast of Vancouver Island. They winter on both coastlines of the Americas, with the largest southern concentrations along the desert-backed beaches of Peru and Chile.

ADRIAN DORST

56 **SHOREBIRDS**

TIMING OF MIGRATION: EARLY BIRDS

Not only is there a geographic shape to the shorebird migration, there is a temporal shape. Migration usually occurs in waves. The first wave often consists of failed breeders and nonbreeders. Some of the latter may have summered south of the breeding grounds. The first breeders to depart the nesting grounds are normally the females, which have spent the most energy in producing the eggs and therefore have a higher stake in arriving at the staging area first. They are followed by the males and then the juveniles. The greater the distance between breeding and wintering grounds, the more likely it is that one parent will depart the breeding grounds early. The reason for this staggered migration was once thought to relate to diminishing food supplies on the tundra. A parent deserted the young in order to make available more food for its progeny. However, there appears to be more than enough food for everyone on the tundra, even late in the arctic summer. More likely, the early desertion increases the chances of survival for the adult, by allowing more time for fattening on the staging grounds. It's a case of the early bird getting the worm.

At many stopover sites, successive waves of shorebirds steadily deplete their prey as the migratory season wears on. In a study conducted by the Manomet Observatory for Conservation Sciences in Plymouth, Massachusetts, reseachers showed that the number of invertebrate prey dropped dramatically, from 7 to 90 per cent, during the staging period. Seasonal production of food resources and competition, then, may be very important factors in shaping migratory patterns of shorebirds. Due to seasonal productivity, food is available at certain sites at very precise times of the year. Individuals who inherit the behavioural and physiological equipment to be in the right place at the right time are favoured. Although it has yet to be proven, it follows that birds that arrive at these prime locations late in the season, or in poorer condition, would have less chance of survival.

One cannot witness the frenetic feeding of the shorebirds at their staging areas without sensing the urgency of their mission. I always watch, with a mixture of bemusement and admiration, as the sandpipers scurry across the tidal flats of the Bay of Fundy stabbing the surface relentlessly to glean its rich harvest of mudshrimp. The birds seem to know that they must lay on as much fat as quickly as possible in preparation for the imminent seventy-hour, nonstop flight to South America over perilous waters.

A semipalmated plover strikes a wary pose on its breeding grounds near Churchill, Manitoba. It exhibits the large head and eyes typical of plovers. ARTHUR MORRIS/BIRDS AS ART

WINTERING SITES: GOING SOUTH

Not all shorebirds migrate as far as Central and South America. Many winter in coastal and interior areas of the United States and northern Mexico. Several species, such as the western sandpiper, long- and short-billed dowitchers, the dunlin, the snowy plover, and the long-billed curlew, concentrate in coastal areas of the Gulf of Mexico, especially in south Florida.

The majority, however, reach the Neotropics, in Central and South America. In the 1980s, Guy Morrison and his Canadian Wildlife Service colleague Ken Ross flew 28 000 kilometres (17,000 miles) of the South American coastline to pinpoint the exact destinations of these northern breeders. They counted nearly 3 million shorebirds. Perhaps not surprisingly, since it is the first landfall, the north coast of South America was the most important wintering area, harbouring 2.5 million, or 86 per cent of the South American total. The Guianas—Guyana, Suriname (the former Dutch Guiana), and French Guiana—accounted for three-quarters of these. The balance was divided almost equally between the Atlantic and Pacific coasts.

Eighty per cent of the shorebirds counted in South America were small sandpipers. Most shorebirds on the north coast were peeps, with semipalmated sandpipers predominating. Farther to the south, along the Atlantic coast of Tierra del Fuego, white-rumped sandpipers were more common, occurring on rocky *restingas*. On the Pacific coast, sanderlings string out along the desert-backed beaches of Chile and Peru. Western sandpipers—that other great tribe of peeps—appear to winter north of the South American continent, primarily in Panama.

The half-million medium-sized shorebirds sighted by the Canadian biologists congregated in two primary areas. Black-bellied plovers and ruddy turnstones preferred the rich intertidal sediments of the coastlines of the Guianas and Brazil. Also, 90 per cent of the yellowlegs concentrated in the Guianas, as did short-billed dowitchers, which exploit mangrove coasts with either extensive mud flats or coastal lagoon systems. Red knots, however, dropped to the bottom of the continent, along the coastlines of Tierra del Fuego and Patagonia, where they find sufficient reserves of mollusks to overwinter. More than half of the South American population is concentrated in the Bahia Lomas, near the eastern end of the Strait of Magellan. This area contains vast expanses of smooth and channelled mud flats backed by flat grasslands.

Whither the large shorebirds? Morrison and Ross found that they disperse to a number of centres—in Suriname, on the north-central coast of Brazil, in Tierra del Fuego, and

FACING PAGE: *This American oystercatcher engages in a dramatic aggressive display on its home territory of Baja California, Mexico. A strictly coastal species, it migrates only short distances, if at all.* ART WOLFE

*A flock of black-necked stilts gather
on their wintering grounds in
Venezuela. Some of this unmistakable species also winter in the
extreme south of the United States.*
ART WOLFE

This migratory flock of whimbrels is shown in Clayoquot Sound, British Columbia. Whimbrels concentrate in winter near Chiloe, Chile, and along the north-central coast of Brazil. ADRIAN DORST

in the Chiloe area of southern Chile. The most important area for willets was the mangrove coastline of north-central Brazil, near the mouth of the Amazon. Morrison and Ross were delighted to discover 20,000 Hudsonian godwits on the vast mud flats of Bahia San Sebastian, an enormous bay enclosed by an 18 kilometre (11 mile) shingle spit in the Tierra del Fuego region of Argentina. This was probably the same contingent that we observed passing through James Bay. Another high-density pocket of godwits was found on the Pacific coast near Chiloe Island. Whimbrels, though widely distributed in South America, also concentrated near Chiloe, with its marshy deltas and associated mud flats. The north-central coast of Brazil also held nearly half the 25,000 whimbrels counted by Morrison and Ross.

FACING PAGE: *A flock of greater yellowlegs gather on wintering grounds in New Mexico. Others fly farther south, to Central and South America.* ART WOLFE/TONY STONE WORLDWIDE

RISKS OF MIGRATION:
TALON, OCEAN, MOUNTAIN, AND HUMAN

The year after I flew "the migratory highway" with Morrison and Ross, I returned to James Bay. This time, I joined a survey crew on the ground, at Ekwan Point, halfway up the west coast. Each morning, after liberally applying insect repellant to combat the miasma of biting insects, we walked a transect, identifying birds by sight and sound.

One day, I walked north with retired teacher and naturalist Bob Curry, who then boasted the second-longest bird list in Ontario. We followed a beach ridge luxuriant with sea lime grass. It shimmered like a maritime crop of wheat; beach peas popped underfoot; and the smell of wild strawberries wafted up. "You could last a while up here this time of year," Curry mused. "It's an unforgiving land most of the year, but right now it's bountiful." By dint of their numbers, it was a sentiment shared by the shorebirds gathered there.

Plump profiles of Hudsonian godwits came into focus on the intertidal flats. A flock of 150 red knots wheeled above us, their cinnamon-coloured bellies flashing against the blue like large autumn leaves twisting brilliantly in the air. In this northern wilderness, the only sounds, besides our own footfalls and breathing, were the songs of songbirds, the trumpeting of sandhill cranes, and the restless chirring of shorebirds, which Curry identified with uncanny accuracy and aplomb: "Pectoral sandpiper . . . ruddy turnstone . . . semipalmated plovers . . . greater yellowlegs."

We were headed for the end of the spit which formed a migrant trap. "Fantasy Island," was what Curry had dubbed it, reflecting his hope that we would find something rare and exotic there, something to add to his list.

What both Curry and I secretly wished for was the sighting of an Eskimo curlew, for it was near here, at North Point, that one of the last definitive sightings of this endangered shorebird had been made. I broached the subject.

"Chances of intersecting a curlew in space and time are not very good," Curry admitted.

Statistics grimly bear out the truth of this statement: the Eskimo curlew has been reported in only twenty-five years since 1945, usually in ones and twos, though twenty-one were reported near Galveston Bay, Texas, in 1981, reviving hopes that the little curlew might yet escape extinction. Recently, a conservation organization, Wetlands for the Americas, coordinated a concerted search for Eskimo curlews on their wintering grounds in the pampas of southern Argentina, in their traditional breeding grounds in the Northwest Territories, and at their migratory stopover in Labrador. They failed to turn up a single one. There now may be so few birds that not only can researchers not find them, they simply cannot find each other.

We walked on in silence. Finally we reached the end of the spit—Fantasy Island. There was no curlew. But this arm of the bay had caught and held a flock of three hundred dunlins, fresh arrivals from the north. "They're coming in," observed Curry with satisfaction. The red backs of their breeding plummage were colourful dabs on the bay's murky palette. The dunlins would rest here long enough to moult, replacing their tattered flight feathers in preparation for the long journey ahead.

Seeing the gregarious shorebirds, gathered in great numbers at refuelling stations along their migratory highway, I thought how easy it is to forget that it is not flocks that migrate but individuals. Although they find safety, direction, and perhaps even solace in numbers, it is individual birds that must brook the many risks along the route in order to pass along their unique set of genes. They must face formidable natural hazards, such as freak storms over the oceans, the thin, glacial air of mountain tops, and the falcon's talons. Also, they must brook the hazards wrought by humans. In the past, they had to run a gauntlet of guns. Today, they are met with the sudden alteration of critical habitat throughout the Americas.

ABOVE: *A lone dunlin, displaying the black belly-patch typical of breeding season, rests among a flock of short- and long-billed dowitchers along their coastal migratory route.* ADRIAN DORST

PAGE 68: *The Copper River delta, near Cordova, Alaska, is the most important shorebird site in the Americas, hosting more than 20 million shorebirds during the migration period.* ADRIAN DORST

Part 3

CONSERVING SHOREBIRD OASES

CONSERVING SHOREBIRD OASES

The time to save a species is while it's still common.

—Rosalie Edge, 1907–1962

It is a sight that never fails to inspire wonder: I watch as 200,000 semipalmated sandpipers lift en masse, as if the beach had sprouted wings. They spiral into the air, an avian helix, then work their choreographic splendour over the muddy waters of the upper Bay of Fundy.

These peeps produce their own sound-and-light show as they stream through the clear August air, their wingbeats an audible cloud. First, they are a low-lying nimbostratus cloud scudding over the waves, but as they bank—all at once, as if the flock was a single body—they turn their bright undersides to the sun, and suddenly become a myriad of mirrors, flashing their bold presence, then occulting as they again roll and show their dark backs.

The birds fly wing to wing, performing aerial acrobatics that mock our own feeble efforts in the skies—a half-million wings, almost touching, manoeuvring in perfect unison. The flock becomes aerial protoplasm, a living fog, flowing and coalescing. Finally, the flock settles again like a sheet shaken out and let fall on the beach. There, the chirring birds huddle together, each bird with its beak tucked under a wing, and balanced on one foot to conserve the precious energy they have come here to accumulate. The sandpipers again become beach stone, so ingeniously camouflaged that the uninitiated could drive by and not know they were in the presence of one of the great wonders of the avian world.

FACING PAGE: *American oyster-catchers and short-billed dowitchers stand guard over the tranquillity of a marsh pond in New Jersey. Protecting such wetlands is critical to shorebirds' conservation.* ARTHUR MORRIS/BIRDS AS ART

*Rock sandpipers gather at the north-
ern shorebird oasis of Kachemak
Bay, Alaska.* DANIEL J.
COX/NATURAL EXPOSURES

STAGING SITES: A MOVABLE FEAST

Between 1.5 and 2 million shorebirds congregate at a few select sites in the upper Bay of Fundy annually on their autumnal migration to the Neotropics. Although some thirty-four shorebird species pass through here, 95 per cent of the birds are semipalmated sandpipers. Depending on the year, this constitutes half to 95 per cent of the world total for this species. The Bay of Fundy is but one of a number of estuaries and bays in North America that host enormous shorebird flocks, numbering in the millions. Every May, Delaware Bay becomes a shorebird mecca, as do San Francisco Bay, California; Grays Harbor, Washington; and Boundary Bay, British Columbia.

The most spectacular congregation of shorebirds occurs near the top of the Pacific flyway, on the shallow estuaries, marshes, and tidal flats of the Copper River delta near Cordova, Alaska. This is possibly the most important shorebird concentration site in the world, with as many as 1 million shorebirds having been counted there at one time. During the two- to five-week migration period, more than 20 million shorebirds will rest and recharge here for the last 1000 kilometres (600 miles) of their journey to breeding grounds in the high Arctic. Half are western sandpipers and dunlins—nearly the entire populations of these species in the Pacific flyway. But shorebirds of all sizes—some thirty-six species—converge here: sanderlings, least sandpipers, long-billed and short-billed dowitchers, lesser golden plovers and black-bellied plovers, surfbirds, red knots, and turnstones, both ruddy and black. Like a late spring blizzard, they whirl above and settle upon the generous gift of the Copper River's glacial outwash. Even such rare birds as bristle-thighed curlews gather at this northern oasis in astonishing numbers.

As you watch these majestic flocks, it is easy to be lulled into a false sense of security about the health of shorebird populations. Then it strikes you: the very fact that such a great proportion of the world population of one species is gathered in one place at one time makes it extraordinarily vulnerable to environmental perturbation—whether catastrophic or chronic in nature. Perhaps the most chilling example is the *Exxon Valdez* disaster of March 1989, which missed fouling the Copper River delta by a mere 50 kilometres (30 miles).

To migrating shorebirds, these staging areas—"fat stations," as shorebird biologist Peter Hicklin has dubbed them—are essential to the successful completion of their life cycle. In such fecund places, sky, water, and earth unite, as if by some alchemy, to yield a biological cornucopia, and for the ornithologically and spiritually inclined, a transcendent flight. To most people, mud and marsh are an inhospitable barrens. Such an

FACING PAGE: *The surfbird is a rock shorebird, which feeds on mussels, barnacles, and limpets along the surf-washed, rocky shoreline. It breeds in the alpine tundra of central Alaska and the Yukon.*
ADRIAN DORST

anthropocentric view, however, directly contradicts shorebird perception. The shorebirds' view of the hemisphere is of a vast barrens—an ecological desert—linked by a series of wetland oases. These critical habitats have special characteristics that make them uniquely capable of supporting huge concentrations of shorebirds. For a short time they produce a vast surfeit of food, and shorebirds have evolved to take advantage of these sudden spikes of productivity. The case of Delaware Bay dramatically illustrates this principle.

Every May, a primeval phenomenon draws, with the power of a global magnet, a half-million shorebirds to a stretch 160 kilometres (100 miles) along the New Jersey and Delaware coastlines: semipalmated sandpipers from Suriname, sanderlings from Peru and Chile, ruddy turnstones from Brazil, and red knots from Tierra del Fuego. The shorebirds arrive here with unerring punctuality, exactly in synchrony with an ancient armada— 1 million horseshoe crabs that come ashore to lay their eggs on the sandy beaches of Delaware Bay. Horseshoe crabs are as primitive as they look, claiming an impressive pedigree of 300 million years. The hoof-shaped head region gives them their name (New Jersey fishers sometimes call them "horsefeet"); they also sport a sharp tail, which native Americans used as spear points. More closely related to ancient sea scorpions than to contemporary crabs, these ancient invertebrates create an eerie spectacle as they beach themselves under a full moon. They jostle for space, excavating shallow nests where they deposit their green, tapioca-sized eggs. Tidal action and successive waves of crabs unearth

Every spring, horseshoe crabs come ashore in Delaware Bay to lay their eggs, which fuel the northward migration of red knots and ruddy turnstones. FRED BRUEMMER

some nests, spreading a luxuriant feast for the shorebirds and seabirds. And what a feast! The shorebirds consume an estimated 106 tonnes (117 tons) of crabs' eggs.

Delaware Bay harbours the largest number of horseshoe crabs along the entire east coast of the United States, underscoring the unique character of such stopover, or staging, areas. Nowhere else can be found such an accessible storehouse of energy. The bay not only produces massive amounts of food but does so at precisely the time that shorebirds require it to complete a stage of their annual cycle. Individuals return to the site year after year, and generations of a species have become dependent upon it. More than half of the *rufa* subspecies of knots are to be found in Delaware Bay every May, for instance. They accumulate sufficient fat not only to fuel their northward flight but also to help them survive the initial period on their high arctic nesting grounds, where they are often greeted with snow cover.

Shorebirds follow what Brian Harrington of the Manomet Observatory for Conservation Sciences, Massachusetts, has called a "movable feast." They concentrate at far-flung sites where food production is high enough to fuel the next leg of their migration. It is this tendency for significant proportions of a whole population to concentrate at a single site that makes shorebirds vulnerable. As shorebird biologist J. P. Myers has observed, "It breaks the normal link between the abundance of a species and its immunity to extinction." Normally, enough individuals of an abundant species would never occur in a single place for the population to be at risk. But shorebirds' strategy of congregating at food-rich oases removes this hedge against extinction. These staging areas are geographic bottlenecks, making whole populations vulnerable to local disturbances. This vulnerability was made abundantly clear in the 1800s when hunters lay in wait to harvest huge flocks of the larger shorebirds. Such unsporting hunting practices, when a single volley felled dozens of birds, brought a number of the larger shorebird species close to extinction. In a single day in 1821, two hundred gunners in New Orleans harvested 48,000 lesser golden plovers (at that time known as the American golden plover).

DECLINING SHOREBIRD POPULATIONS

With the lesser golden plover, the Eskimo curlew was once among the most abundant of North American birds, numbering in the millions. Its spring migration through the Great Plains earned it the sobriquet "prairie pigeon." Like those of the passenger pigeon, its flights literally blackened the skies. And like the passenger pigeon, the Eskimo curlew was the victim of a commercial hunt that a century ago brought it to the brink of extinction, where it has teetered ever since. The scale of the killings is difficult to comprehend, impossible to condone. It is reported that curlews were "slaughtered by the wagonload," and when the hunting was particularly good the wagons would be dumped so that curlew bodies "formed piles as large as a couple of tons of coal." These were allowed to rot while the hunters refilled their wagons with "fresh victims."

The Migratory Bird Treaty Act of 1918 effectively removed the threat of hunting to most shorebird populations in Canada and the United States. Subsequently, many populations of shorebirds, with the exception of the Eskimo curlew, rebounded, though few to historic levels. Hunting remains a factor, however, in some places and for some species. Hunters in North America continue to harvest 500,000 common snipe and as many American woodcock every year. Both species are in decline in parts of their range. Hunting is also a continuing problem in isolated pockets of the shorebirds' wintering areas. "Gentlemen's" hunting clubs in Barbados are reported to shoot 15,000 lesser yellowlegs annually. Sport hunting by Europeans also has been revived on the Argentine pampas. Some small shorebirds, such as semipalmated sandpipers, are taken for food in the Guianas, and whimbrels are likewise harvested in parts of northern Brazil and Chile. Nevertheless, hunting is perhaps the least important danger shorebirds now face.

Development in the twentieth century has raised a new gauntlet of risks that shorebirds must run. Most are linked to the degradation of wetland habitat through industrial, agricultural, and recreational activities.

In the last two decades, shorebird populations have been declining on a continent-wide scale. Sixteen of the forty-one common North American shorebird species have shown steady population declines of 3 to 12 per cent annually. Red knots have suffered cumulative reductions of more than 75 per cent, which are the largest declines of a common North American bird species recorded in the twentieth century. Surveys of twelve species conducted along the Atlantic seaboard from Maine to Florida showed a significant reduction in short-billed dowitchers, sanderlings, and whimbrels, as well as less dramatic but disturbing drops in the numbers of black-bellied plovers. Similar surveys at east coast

FACING PAGE: *A lone whimbrel teeters on a tree top, silhouetted by the moon. Its genus name,* Numenius, *means "new moon," in folklore a time of darkness and hauntings. The whimbrel itself is threatened by declining populations in the eastern part of its range.*
G. FONTAINE

PAGES 80–81: *A black-bellied plover in drab winter attire takes shelter in the lee of beach grass on Long Island, New York. Numbers of black-bellied plovers are declining along the Atlantic seaboard.* TOM VEZO

Canadian sites indicated that twenty species (45 per cent of the shorebirds that regularly occur here) were decreasing in some part of their range. Counts declined in the St. Lawrence estuary and Gulf of St. Lawrence as well as in the James Bay and Hudson Bay regions. Significant declines were consistently recorded during the period 1974–91 for semipalmated sandpipers, least sandpipers, and short-billed dowitchers. Decreases for black-bellied plovers and red knots, though not as pronounced, were also observed. Population declines have also been noted for a number of species in the Pacific flyway.

The most precipitous declines occurred during the late 1970s, with an upswing in numbers during the first half of the 1980s, followed by another, though less marked, decline in recent years. It can be a complex problem sorting out whether these changes are part of natural population fluctuations or are induced by human disturbance. A series of cold summers on the breeding grounds in the 1970s may have accounted for the population declines at that time. Similarly, decreased nesting success of semipalmated sandpipers in Manitoba during the 1980s was due to poor local environmental conditions, including late snow melt and cold spring weather. However, most shorebird species disperse widely on the breeding grounds, making them less susceptible to local influences, whether natural or human. As well, the abundance of insect larvae hatched in the tundra environment and the extended feeding times afforded by the long daylight hours make food less of a concern, despite the energy demands of breeding season.

Most natural mortality of adult birds that occurs on the breeding grounds is due to severe weather, which can cause catastrophic losses, as occurred with red knots and ruddy turnstones when a late spring storm swept Ellesmere Island in 1974. Bad weather on the breeding grounds can also cause loss of eggs or young and, in some years, prevent breeding entirely. Even under ideal conditions, shorebirds only produce a small clutch of eggs, usually four or less, so that survival of the adults becomes extremely important to the population as a whole.

If they survive their first year, shorebirds enjoy relatively long lives: the largest species can live for thirty years; medium-sized species, ten to twenty years; whereas the smallest "peeps" probably live fewer than ten years, and perhaps only four or five years on average. Survivorship of adults is indeed high, between 70 and 95 per cent every year. Therefore, any factors that endanger the adult birds when they are away from the breeding grounds become extremely important to the welfare of the population as a whole.

At first, shorebird biologists thought that the declines they were observing were part of a long-term cycle of normal population fluctuations. "But now it's twenty years, and still going," says Brian Harrington. "I'm beginning to become very concerned, because I've seen these trends are not reversing, they're not changing. And I think there is some very real problem and it's having an enormous effect on populations—and we don't really have a good clue as to what it is."

ABOVE: *A ruddy turnstone incubates its clutch of eggs on Rowley Island, North-west Territories. Bad weather in the high Arctic can cause catastrophic losses of adults and young.* JAN VAN DE KAM

FACING PAGE: *Shorebirds normally produce a clutch of four eggs, such as these sandpiper eggs nestled among an arctic nosegay in the Alaska National Wildlife Refuge.* ART WOLFE

HABITAT LOSS: DISAPPEARING WETLANDS

There are a number of factors, alone and in combination, that could be responsible for declining populations: habitat loss, pollution, and human disturbance. Without question, wetland loss has affected shorebirds to the greatest degree. In wintering and staging areas, shorebirds use food resources to the limit. In brutally simple terms, then, the drying up of wetlands has meant fewer shorebirds. It may even be that the shorebirds' risky behaviour of concentrating in such huge numbers at staging areas is a relatively new strategy forced upon them by declining options—there simply may be nowhere else to go.

The draining, ditching, infilling, and diking of wetlands have degraded or removed much shorebird habitat throughout North America. Within the United States 46 per cent of coastal and interior wetlands have already been lost, and they continue to be destroyed at the rate of almost half a hectare (an acre) per minute. A third of Canada's wetlands also have been dried up.

This onslaught on wetlands followed immediately upon the arrival of Europeans on the continent. In the Bay of Fundy, French settlers brought dike-building technology with them to the New World in the early seventeenth century, and by the beginning of the twentieth century 90 per cent of the salt marshes had been converted to agricultural production. Similarly, ditching for mosquito control had affected 90 per cent of the tidelands from Maine to Virginia by 1938.

Eighty per cent of the U.S. population now lives in a band 80 kilometres (50 miles) from the shoreline along the Pacific, Gulf, and Atlantic coastlines. Residential and recreational development on the barrier islands along the coasts of New Jersey and Delaware has consumed much of this maritime wetland and promises to do the same along the coasts of Texas, Florida, and Louisiana. There has been a similar pattern of wetland degradation along the Pacific coast. Fully 91 per cent of California's wetlands have been lost. Urbanization has consumed 85 per cent of San Francisco Bay's tidal wetlands since the 1950s and is continuing to carve away and fragment the remaining habitat. Dredging and filling activities threaten critical sites within the Grays Harbor estuary, Washington.

Wetlands have fared no better in the interior, where water has been siphoned off for agricultural purposes. Overall, in the United States, approximately 80 per cent of freshwater wetlands have been lost. In particular, the introduction of deep irrigation, utilizing the centre-pivot system, has lowered the water table over large areas, causing changes to surface water and vegetation. This, in combination with a drought, resulted, in 1989, in the virtual drying up of Cheyenne Bottoms wetland in Kansas, an area of 17 000 hectares

FACING PAGE: *A New York commuter train bears down on a winter flock of dunlins. Human disturbance—industrial, residential, and recreational—may be a major cause of declining shorebird populations.*
ARTHUR MORRIS/BIRDS AS ART

(41,000 acres) where 50 per cent of all shorebirds migrating through the interior of the United States stop on their spring and autumn migrations.

In the Great Plains states, an average of half of the wetlands, including 57 per cent of the pothole wetlands in North and South Dakota, have been lost. These ephemeral and dynamic habitats are perhaps the most endangered wetlands in the continental United States. In addition, half of the upland grassland in prairie pothole country of the northern United States and Canada is now under cultivation for corn and grain, significantly reducing the range of prairie-nesting shorebirds such as the American avocet, long-billed curlew, willet, marbled godwit, and mountain plover.

Mountain plovers present an interesting case study of the dismantling of this ecosystem and the interdependencies that sustained shorebird populations on the Great Plains. Historically, mountain plovers nested on short-grass prairie, where bison and prairie dog activity kept vegetation sparse. By 1914, the eradication of the buffalo and prairie dogs, along with widespread cultivation, had sent the mountain plover population plummeting. Their wintering habitat has also been destroyed in the Central Valley of California, where 90 per cent of the seasonally flooded wetlands have been converted to agriculture, further reducing the continental population to between 5000 and 15,000 birds in the last quarter-century.

Water has also been diverted to sustain growing urban populations. Mono Lake, California, the source of Los Angeles's drinking water, has suffered most. In his novel *Roughing It,* Mark Twain erroneously dubbed this important shorebird oasis, high in the Sierras, "the dead sea of California." In fact, the salty waters and glaring alkali flats support a seething, buzzing abundance of brine shrimp and alkali flies—food for 90,000 Wilson's phalaropes and 150,000 red-necked phalaropes that fatten here before embarking on their southward migration. Since 1941, four of the lake's six feeder streams have been diverted to supply water to Los Angeles, causing the lake level to drop 14 metres (45 feet). As a result, the lake's salt content has doubled, endangering the fragile ecosystem and the shorebirds and other waterbirds that depend upon it. Injunctions filed by the U.S. Forest Service to restore water flow to the lake have won the lake and its birds a reprieve. The goal is to raise the lake level over the next twenty to thirty years.

Modest gains have also been made for wetlands in Canada and the United States in the last several years, thanks to the North American Waterfowl Management Plan. Significant wetland restoration, especially of marginal farmland in prairie pothole country, was designed to improve waterfowl breeding habitat. It should also benefit temperate-breeding shorebirds, such as the marbled godwit, American avocet, common snipe, Wilson's phalarope, red-necked phalarope, and willet. However, these are not the species in decline. Although the habitat improvement seems to have boosted waterfowl numbers

significantly, those shorebird species in decline have continued their downward trend. Brian Harrington believes that reasons for the declines are to be found at the migration stopover sites and wintering areas where birds concentrate. Effects there are more likely to have population-wide consequences than are effects on the breeding grounds or on wintering grounds where populations are more dispersed. Both pollutants and chronic human disturbance warrant increased scrutiny as two possible causes of the dramatic declines.

Western sandpipers and dowitchers congregate at Bowerman Basin, Washington, an important stopover on the Pacific flyway. ART WOLFE

POLLUTANTS: TOXIC THREAT

Oil pollution poses an ever-present threat to a number of the major staging areas. The *Exxon Valdez* spill in western Prince William Sound was as close to an apocalyptic disaster for shorebirds as has occurred to date. The 3 million barrels of spilled crude washed ashore a mere 50 kilometres (30 miles) from the adjacent Copper River delta, in the eastern portion of the sound. If the tides and winds had carried the oil southward into the delta, it might have been disastrous for a number of populations, including dunlins and western sandpipers. The glaciated mountain ranges rising from the sea along the Pacific northwest coast of British Columbia and southeastern Alaska leave little or no suitable alternative feeding or resting areas for shorebirds along this coast. As well, rafts of 50,000 red-necked phalaropes forage at sea directly in the path of the major tanker route into and out of the Valdez terminus of the Trans Alaska Oil Pipeline. If the spill had occurred two months later, many of these birds would have suffered fatal oiling. Annually, ten thousands of surfbirds and black turnstones—significant fractions of the world population for these species—gather to gorge on herring roe that washes ashore on islands within Prince William Sound, a phenomenon analogous to the horseshoe crab egg orgy in Delaware Bay. A shift of 10 to 15 kilometres (5 to 10 miles) in the trajectory of the spill could have doomed these birds and fouled their feeding grounds.

Delaware Bay is the largest oil transfer port of entry on the east coast of the United States. With billions of barrels of oil received annually, it is vulnerable to a spill. Emergency plans have been developed, but they would only be effective in dealing with relatively small spills, and even then under fairly benign weather conditions. Likewise, in the Gulf of Mexico, the Houston Ship Channel—the intercoastal waterway supplying the largest oil port in the United States—skirts the Bolivar Flats Reserve, which is an important staging site as well as wintering area for short-billed dowitchers, American avocets, and the endangered piping plover. Offshore drilling and loading of tankers also imperils the Bahia San Sebastian region of Tierra del Fuego, which harbours half of the continental population of Hudsonian godwits in winter, as well as significant numbers of red knots.

Whereas oil probably presents the most acute threat to shorebird populations, a host of other synthetic, oil-based organic compounds pose a chronic problem for shorebirds as well as other bird groups, including the raptors that prey upon them. These compounds were developed in chemical warfare laboratories but found use in the civilian world when it was discovered they acted on insects as well as humans.

FACING PAGE: *Coastal pulp and paper plants such as this pose a toxic threat to shorebirds. Synthetic chlorine compounds—so-called organochlorines—are particularly worrisome as they accumulate at ever higher doses in the food web.*
GRAHAM OSBORNE

Many of these organic (carbon-based) compounds contain chlorine. These so-called organochlorines, or chlorinated hydrocarbons, inhibit the action of essential neurotransmitters—the chemical messengers that carry impulses in the nervous system—of insects as well as higher animals. They knock down insects but, in sufficient doses, also birds, fish, and mammals. In the case of insects, this was the desired effect. But these chlorinated compounds had unanticipated long-term effects because of their stable chemical structure. They simply do not break down in the environment. They accumulate and concentrate at ever higher doses in the food web—a process called biomagnification. Although levels might be nearly undetectable in water, plants growing in the water accumulate the chemicals in their tissues. Plant-eaters further concentrate these compounds, storing them in their fat. Predators, including fishes and birds of prey, ultimately receive the highest doses from their food sources. The concentration of these persistent compounds is like an inverted pyramid, with levels in the predators sometimes escalating to millions of times those found in the organisms at the bottom of the food chain.

At sufficient levels—mere parts per million—such compounds are toxic enough to be fatal. But they also have indirect impacts on bird populations. The most notorious of these compounds is the insecticide DDT. It was banned in North America in the 1970s, when it was discovered that it prevented the proper metabolism of calcium, resulting in eggshell thinning. Eggs collapsed and with them populations of eagles, hawks, and fish-eating seabirds such as gannets.

Peregrine falcons, which prey heavily upon shorebirds, were one of the species most affected. This directed concern at shorebirds themselves, which, to no one's surprise, were found to harbour significant levels of these persistent compounds. Studies carried out on the south Texas coast in 1980, eight years after the ban on DDT use in the United States, showed significant levels of chlorinated pesticides—DDE (the toxic breakdown product of DDT), dieldrin (forty to fifty times as toxic as DDT), and toxaphene, a persistent toxin used to control cotton boll weevils in the lower Rio Grande Valley of Texas. Canals that drained thousands of hectares of cotton and sorghum cropland carried their contaminant-laden runoff into the Laguna Madre, a wintering area on the Gulf of Mexico for thousands of migratory shorebirds. Long-billed dowitchers and American avocets accumulated levels of these contaminants high enough to impair reproduction.

Pesticide application may be of greater concern in the wintering areas of South America, where agriculture is expanding rapidly and controls on pesticide application, including DDT, are generally less stringent, or in some instances nonexistent. Organochlorine residues have been found in a wide variety of wintering shorebirds in Peru, Ecuador, and Suriname. The highest levels of DDE—in lesser yellowlegs, spotted sandpipers, and semipalmated plovers—were recorded in Peru and may be related to the continued use of DDT for pest control in the Lima area.

Unfortunately, there is not much data on contaminants in North American shorebirds wintering south of the equator. The most extensive studies have been carried out in the rice fields of coastal Suriname, which have become important winter feeding areas for some species, particularly least sandpipers and greater and lesser yellowlegs. Pesticides and herbicides are sprayed almost continuously throughout the year for the control of weeds, snails, and insects. Black-bellied plovers, white-rumped sandpipers, and least sandpipers are perhaps most at risk because they tend to forage in fields that have been sprayed recently.

The implications are widespread because the commercially successful Wageningen project in Suriname has become a model for rice-growing operations not only elsewhere in Central and South America but also along the Gulf of Mexico coast and in California.

Agriculture is not solely to blame for pollution of shorebird habitat. Industry has sluiced its share of organic and inorganic chemicals into the continent's waterways and coastal regions. Two-thirds of factories producing pesticides and other synthetic organic chemicals, 60 per cent of those producing inorganic chemicals, 50 per cent of the petroleum-refining plants, and two-thirds of pulp mills are located in coastal areas. Investigators are currently looking into contamination of horseshoe crab eggs, including the presence of polychlorinated biphenyls (PCBs), which are carcinogenic, in Delaware Bay, and there are similar concerns about contamination from agricultural, urban, and industrial runoff in the San Franscisco Bay area.

Mining also contributes its share of contaminants, in particular heavy metals, which, like organochlorines, accumulate and concentrate in fat tissues. Whimbrels feed on an intertidal area where heavy metal-laden tailings were deposited from the El Salvador copper-mining operation in the Chanaral region of northern Chile; these birds accumulated a toxic dose of cadmium—also a concern for the region's people, who commonly hunt whimbrels.

One of the worst toxic sinks is Utah's Great Salt Lake, an area of hemispheric importance to shorebirds. Dozens of industries rimming the saline lake have used it as a dumping ground for a variety of heavy metals, including lead, and other toxic elements such as arsenic and selenium. These pollutants are further concentrated by natural evaporation. Evaporation ponds for the extraction of minerals can concentrate even the lake's natural salts to lethal levels. Salt sticks to the wings of migrating birds, preventing them from flying. Stranded, they ultimately die of thirst.

A wide variety of persistent toxins—both organochlorines and heavy metals—also were found in shorebirds wintering on the mud flats and bays of Corpus Christi, Texas. Here, a complex of oil refineries, zinc smelters, and chemical plants add their pollutants to agricultural runoff from nearby farmlands. The shorebirds contained relatively low levels of individual organochlorines and heavy metals, though levels of selenium (a nonmetallic by-product of the smelting industry) were high enough to inhibit reproduction. Levels of individual toxins were not high enough to warrant concern by themselves, but it is not known how the components of this chemical stew might combine to produce ill effects on individual birds and populations. Unfortunately, the shorebirds at Corpus Christi are the rule rather than the exception in carrying a heavy burden of potentially toxic chemicals.

The peculiar ecology of shorebirds as long-distance migrants makes them particularly susceptible to these persistent toxins. Both organochlorines and heavy metals accumulate in fat. It is to be expected that shorebirds, with their need for storing fat reserves, should also become repositories of these fat-soluble compounds. As long as the compounds are sequestered in the fat tissue, there are few problems. During migration, however, shorebirds burn off these reserves of fat very quickly—in forty to eighty hours. Many biologists wonder what happens to the birds when these toxic substances are freed into the bloodstream. How do they affect their vital organs, such as the liver and brain, and ultimately their success in migration and reproduction? Such questions, urgent as they are, are impossible to answer with the current data and level of knowledge of the physiological effects of pollutants.

FACING PAGE: *The loss of interior wetlands and cultivation of upland grassland for corn and grain has significantly reduced the breeding grounds of prairie-nesting shorebirds such as this long-billed curlew.*
DAVID WEINTRAUB

HUMAN DISTURBANCE

Human disturbance, however, has a more direct and measurable effect on shorebirds. Disturbance forces birds off prime feeding areas and reduces their efficiency in feeding.

Humans are attracted to beaches, lakeshores, and estuaries for a variety of recreational activities. Birders and naturalists go there to observe the birds themselves. Whatever our motives, our presence often causes enough commotion to disturb birds as they go about their routines of feeding, nesting, and roosting.

Recreational activites on beaches have put at least two species of shorebirds, the snowy plover and piping plover, on the endangered list. Both species breed in temperate regions of North America. Unlike the species that breed in the subarctic and Arctic, far from the madding crowds, these pale plovers choose to breed in the places where we ourselves summer. "Beach abuse by folks," to borrow J. P. Myers's phrase, has reduced the breeding population of the snowy plover in central California by more than 90 per cent. Abuse includes all manner of activity, from jogging to a reckless ride in an off-road vehicle. The snowy plover, a delicate bird the colour of its sandy beach habitat, has the unfortunate habit of building its nest on wide berms above the tideline, a narrow strip of habitat that is regularly trodden on by beachcombers and their pets, or, in recent years, has disappeared completely under condominiums and marinas. The fact that a turnaround for the snowy plover will require a change in human behaviour makes its prospects dim. With no recovery plan in place, Myers predicts the snowy plover's imminent demise.

Like the snowy plover, the piping plover makes its nest in the sand, a shallow scrape for its four eggs. Three breeding populations exist: on the Great Plains, from the Prairie provinces to Nebraska; on the Atlantic coast, from Newfoundland to South Carolina; and in the Great Lakes region. The latter population has been completely extirpated from the highly populated lakeshores in Canada, with only a remnant population surviving on offshore islands in Michigan. Populations elsewhere are hanging on, with an estimated 1600 pairs in North America. Human disturbance is clearly the cause of breeding failure. A 50 per cent increase in visitors to Prince Edward Island National Park reduced breeding success there to a mere 14 per cent. Critical beach habitat now has been protected, and similar plans are underway in Massachusetts, Rhode Island, Connecticut, New Jersey, and Virginia. In the Quill Lakes region of Saskatchewan, which hosts 4 per cent of the Great Plains piping plovers, the delay of haying and the fencing of critical areas have helped to protect the beleaguered little plover.

Chronic disturbance may also play a role in the success or failure of long-distance migrants. Watching birds at their stopovers, one can sense their almost desperate need to put on fat. They spread out over the intertidal area, mining it with a manic diligence between high tides. Only when the tide itself rests do the birds rest, on the thin strips of beach that provide roosts. This brief rest period, however, is vital to their purpose of conserving energy for the long flight ahead.

Unfortunately, the southward migration of shorebirds coincides with the outdoor recreation season in North America. In July and August, people and shorebirds often congregate in the same places, at beaches and along lakeshores. While taking routine censuses, Harrington has observed that shorebirds are disturbed by dogs, joggers, kite-fliers, boats, and jet skis. A roosting group of birds might get disturbed as many fifteen or thirty times during a high-tide period.

Harrington has calculated the energetic costs of such constant disturbance, and for the knot it is considerable. Up to a third of their net fat gain each day is burned off in reacting to human recreational activities. "That could have two consequences," surmises Harrington. "It could end up with birds leaving underweight or with birds having to stay longer at a staging area." Either way, it might reduce the chances of a succesful migration.

A parallel study of semipalmated sandpipers appears to confirm Harrington's fears of birds being unable to accumulate sufficient flight fuel. Peeps show a high degree of site fidelity, returning to the same beach year after year. However, those birds departing in the lower 20 to 30 per cent weight category are rarely showing up again in later years. By contrast, 70 to 80 per cent of birds in the higher weight class are returning. "It makes me wonder," says Harrington, "whether these birds [that are not returning] may not be getting up to the weight they need to, and they're dying out over the ocean in the south migration."

A puff of down on legs, no bigger than a clam shell, this piping plover chick is the fragile hope of an endangered species. Other beach-nesting species, such as the snowy plover, also face extinction if "beach abuse by folks" is not curbed. TOM VEZO

TRANSFORMING ECOSYSTEMS

Disturbance is an example of humans inadvertantly altering habitat merely by our presence. With the aid of technology, however, we have the means of deliberately transforming whole ecosystems. Although fewer megaprojects have been proposed in recent years, a number of grandiose schemes remain on the drawing board and, if implemented, could have drastic effects upon shorebird populations. One of the most threatening is the Grand Canal project, which would see the transformation of James Bay from a marine ecosystem into a freshwater reservoir by the construction of a dike 160 kilometres (100 miles) across the top of the bay. Such a project, according to an environmental review, would "most likely destroy a major portion of the North American migratory bird population" that nests, feeds, and moults there. The project was devised to collect freshwater from the Canadian Shield and distribute it to the parched southern and western parts of the continent. In the last two decades, half of the wild rivers on the east side of James Bay already have been dammed for the export of hydroelectricity to the northeastern United States. Proposals to dam the remaining untapped river basins may affect the salinity and nutrient mixture within the bay—with catastrophic impacts on bird life.

Another grandiose scheme to export electricity to New England and New York is Fundy Tidal Power, a perennial engineering dream to exploit the high tides of the Bay of Fundy. The damming of tidal rivers for the protection of dikeland and, in one instance, for the operation of a pilot tidal power plant has already demonstrated profound effects on invertebrate-rich sediments in the bay, transforming these grounds into "biological deserts." Ecosystem-wide changes in the intertidal zone could cause the annihilation of the mudshrimp *(Corophium volutator),* the sediment-sensitive organism that is the foundation for the massive shorebird migrations into the region.

The human mania for the manipulation of water—primarily for irrigation and hydroelectricity—also threatens "the green lagoons" of the Cienega de Santa Clara, the most important wetland in Mexico's Sonoran Desert. Presided over by human-shaped saguaro cacti, the desert spreads its barren beauty northward into Arizona. Much of this wilderness has been domesticated, and further dessicated, by the successive damming of the Colorado River, beginning in 1935 with the Boulder (Hoover) Dam on the Arizona-Nevada border. The diversion of water for desert agriculture in Arizona and California has robbed the river delta of much of its nutrient- and sediment-rich flow into the Golfo de California. Aerial surveys identified this region as an important wintering area for marbled godwits, willets, American avocets, and peeps—annually harbouring 150,000 shorebirds in all. Concern for the shorebirds that flock to these desert oases now centres on whether the Colorado River Basin Salinity Control Project for desalination of irrigation water will return sufficient flows to maintain the Cienega de Santa Clara wetland and the delta habitat downstream.

In South America, the most environmentally ominous water diversion plan is the proposed Hidrovia Project, or Paraguay–Parana Waterway Project. It would transform the second-largest river basin in South America, formed by the Parana River and its major tributary, the Paraguay. The project would convert the wild rivers into a Mississippi-style transportation system 3400 kilometres (2100 miles) long for freighter and barge-train traffic, linking portions of Argentina, Paraguay, Bolivia, and Brazil. At risk is the Pantanal ("the Great Marsh"), the largest continuous wetland system in the world and a region of international significance for biodiversity.

This huge wetland acts as a sponge, absorbing the periodic floods that inundate the La Plata Basin and releasing the water gradually and harmlessly. It functions not only as a natural form of flood control but also as an important feeding and breeding ground for waterfowl and other native waterbirds, and as a migratory highway for shorebirds. Taking these factors into account, Wetlands for the Americas, a nonprofit organization dedicated to the conservation of wetlands and their biodiversity in the Western Hemisphere, has prepared an environmental analysis of the project. The report, called *Hidrovia: An Initial Examination of the Paraguay–Parana Waterway*, questions Hidrovia's overall economic benefits and outlines its potential for exacting high environmental costs:

> Migratory bird species (including shorebirds, ducks, herons, and storks, among others) may suffer from the loss of large areas of suitable habitat due to habitat changes, modifications in the flooding regime, and pollution. The reduction in places for breeding, feeding, and wintering resulting from the shrinkage of wetland habitats at the continent-wide scale, coupled with changes in the hydrological regime, may result in severe population crashes which may put at risk the survival of many species. In fact, given the size and latitudinal extension of the wetlands included in the Paraguay–Parana system, the possibility exists that impacts caused by Hidrovia on migratory birds may well affect bird diversity on a continental scale.

Wetlands for the Americas worries not only about the direct impacts of the project but also about the cumulative impacts of development that the project is designed to foster. Population growth in the basin is likely to increase the negative consequences of deforestation, intense soil erosion, and pollution already taking place there.

The rapid pace of development in South America, and the relative lack of environmental regulations in some countries, threaten important ecosystems and the shorebirds dependent upon them. One of the most productive ecosystems is the grasslands, or pampas, of Argentina and Uruguay. In its pristine state, this open, treeless terrain was attractive to many grassland shorebirds. However, cropping and expanded livestock activities in the last century have drastically altered the vegetation. "Pampas are one of the most threatened ecosystems in South America, because they are so easy to modify," says Pablo Canevari, president of Wetlands for the Americas in South America.

Grassland shorebirds, both migrants and South American species, that depend upon this much-modified habitat have inevitably come under stress. Gone are the days, which William Henry Hudson described in the 1880s, when lesser golden plovers congregated "in such numbers that they blacken the ground over an area of several acres in extent; and at a distance of a quarter of a mile the din of their united voices resembles the roar of a cataract." The plover's flight mate, the Eskimo curlew, may be completely absent from the present-day pampas, the last one having been sighted in Argentina in 1939. An extensive search by forty ornithologists of 11 500 square kilometres (4400 square miles) of the curlew's traditional wintering grounds, in 1992–93, failed to find one, though flocks of other grassland shorebirds, such as lesser golden plover and buff-breasted, upland, and pectoral sandpipers, were fairly common. Although modification of the pampas may have been a contributing factor in the small curlew's fate, North American hunting still seems the more likely cause of its virtual disappearance. However, future development of the pampas, especially agricultural cropping, could put at risk even the more abundant grassland species.

Although not yet as degraded as those in North America, wetlands throughout Latin America are succumbing to rapid development. Urbanization and recreational tourism endanger coastal concentrations of sanderlings and lesser golden plovers in Coquimbo Bay in central Chile and Buenos Aires, Argentina, respectively. Already, most of the wetlands in Uruguay have been converted to rice production. Coastal mangrove systems, which feed and harbour important populations of wintering shorebirds (including spotted sandpipers), are being altered for commercial shrimp farms in Mexico, Central America, and Ecuador. In Ecuador's Gulfo de Guayaquil, shrimp ponds have decimated the highly productive mangrove systems. As well, 15 to 20 per cent of the mangrove wetlands of the Marismas Nacionales area, on the Pacific coast of Mexico, have been destroyed by opening lagoons to the sea in order to provide feeding grounds for shrimp. As well, deforestation and mining in the Amazon Basin is altering the kind and amount of sediments being exported at the river's mouth. The tremendous outflow of Amazon water is swept northwestward, where its sediments (originating in the Andes) are deposited on the huge mud flats of Suriname and French Guiana. It is these same sediments, with their invertebrate riches, that support the massive numbers of wintering shorebirds along the north coast of South America.

It has only been very recently that the importance of wetlands in Central America for shorebirds has been recognized. These wetlands face many of the same problems as those on the southern continent—deforestation and intensive agriculture with the inevitable influx of sediments and agricultural chemicals. The most important shorebird site in Central America is probably the Bahia de Panama. It serves as a critical stopover site for more than fifteen migratory species and may be the most important wintering area for millions of shorebirds that annually migrate to and from the Canadian Arctic. Half of the world's population of western sandpipers is thought to pass through this vast stretch of coastal wetlands and tidal mud flats. Unfortunately, human and industrial pollution from nearby Panama City threatens the integrity of this critical feeding ground.

In the late twentieth century, humans have recognized with a shudder their capacity to alter not only ecosystems but the environment on a global scale. Until recently, the northern breeding grounds of many shorebirds seemed immune from our influence. Global warming, however, could drastically alter the specialized northern habitat that shorebirds journey so far to exploit. Coastal migratory stopovers could also be altered or obliterated, as sea levels rise in response to the greenhouse effect of burgeoning carbon dioxide levels. Models of the greenhouse effect predict less rain for the Great Plains. Drought conditions led to a drying up of Cheyenne Bottoms in 1989, leaving the fate of some 150,000 shorebirds unknown. Such catastrophic breakdowns of major migratory stopovers could become more common in future if trends in greenhouse gases are not reversed.

CONSERVATION EFFORTS: LINKS IN THE CHAIN

Conservation of shorebirds in the Western Hemisphere ultimately depends on protection of the special habitats, principally wetlands, that shorebirds rely on in meeting the energetic demands of their annual cycle. The survey work carried out in the 1970s—the International Shorebird Survey, the Maritime Shorebird Survey, and the Pan-American Shorebird Survey—demonstrated not only that shorebirds concentrate at particular sites but that they employ a series of such sites in completing their transhemispheric travels. Conservationists recognized that to safeguard species it was insufficient to protect one site along the shorebirds' migratory corridor at the neglect of others. Each was a link in a chain. Therefore, protecting Delaware Bay would not ensure survival of red knots if their northern staging area in James Bay or their South American wintering grounds in Argentina were imperilled.

A plan to protect these critical links arose from the long-term research of three visionary shorebird biologists: Brian Harrington of the Manomet Observatory, Massachusetts; J. P. Myers, then affiliated with the National Academy of Sciences, Philadelphia; and Guy Morrison of the Canadian Wildlife Service, Ottawa. Their vision was to see the world as shorebirds do: a global view encompassing the ecological jewels of wetlands—green and shining places—scattered throughout the Western Hemisphere. Conservation of shorebirds, they realized, must be rooted in the shorebirds' cosmopolitan ecology rather than in any artificial, political context.

Formal efforts to conserve critical links in the migratory chain arose independently within the World Wildlife Fund in the United States and the Canadian Wildlife Service. Then, in 1985, the International Association of Fish and Wildlife Agencies (IAFWA)—the federal, state, and provincial games agencies of Canada, the United States, and Mexico—collaborated with the World Wildlife Fund in identifying lands under IAFWA's control, which could form the basis of an international conservation system.

The practical result of these efforts was the birth of the Western Hemisphere Shorebird Reserve Network (WHSRN), a unique consortium of private and public agencies. WHSRN has established biological criteria for the designation of reserves of varying importance. Those hosting more than a half-million shorebirds or 30 per cent of a flyway population are potential hemispheric reserves; international reserves host more than 100,000 birds, or 15 per cent of a flyway population; regional reserves, more than 20,000, or 5 per cent of a population. A further designation has been earmarked for endangered species sites, and in future critical breeding areas may be included. Potential

FACING PAGE: *The upland sandpiper is one of the grassland shorebirds facing challenges in the Southern Hemisphere, where the pampas ecosystem is being transformed by agricultural development.*
WAYNE LYNCH

reserve sites are nominated by the landowner, and their eligibility reviewed every six months by a ten-member WHSRN council. There are currently some two hundred sites under consideration. The first hemispheric reserve to be established was the lower estuary of Delaware Bay, followed by the dedication of two sites in the upper Bay of Fundy. In its first decade, the network has grown to encompass thirty-two sites in seven countries, protecting 30 million shorebirds and about 5 million hectares (12 million acres) of wetlands.

In a concrete expression of its international outlook, WHSRN has also instituted the twinning of so-called sister reserves, which share birds during different phases of their annual cycle. So, the Bay of Fundy has been twinned with the Wia-Wia, Coppename, and Bigi Pan reserves in Suriname, where the majority of semipalmated sandpipers winter. Similarly, Great Salt Lake, Utah; Mono Lake, California; and the saline wetlands of Laguna Mar Chiquita, Argentina—all of which attract and sequester huge populations of the salt-loving Wilson's phalarope—were named sister reserves.

WHSRN membership is voluntary, and management of the site is the prerogative of the landowner. There is nothing legal or binding to the inclusion, but once sites are designated, WHSRN can use the designation as moral suasion. WHSRN has flexed its moral muscle as a lobby group, convincing the United States Congress to appropriate nearly $5 million to acquire water rights at Stillwater National Wildlife Refuge, which hosts 250,000 shorebirds, primarily long-billed dowitchers, western sandpipers, and American avocets. WHSRN also encourages the participation of other agencies involved in wetland protection, such as RAMSAR, the designation for the Convention of Wetlands of International Importance. The first WHSRN reserve to be jointly recognized by RAMSAR and WHSRN was Cheyenne Bottoms, a vital seasonal wetland for 90 per cent of five species of shorebirds passing through the dry western interior of the United States. There is now a movement to make the network global in scope through Wetlands International, a newly formed global partnership heaquartered in the United Kingdom, Malaysia, and Canada.

In North America, WHSRN has brought the concerns of shorebirds under the umbrella of the North American Waterfowl Management Plan, a $1.5 billion, fifteen-year plan to rehabilitate wetlands in the United States and Canada. In the Southern Hemisphere, WHSRN has helped launch the Neotropical Wetlands Program for the protection of wetlands in Central and South America. WHSRN also sponsors field and policy workshops in the region, to raise awareness of shorebird conservation issues and foster research. The hope is that shorebirds, until now a low-profile group, will become a flagship group for the protection of wetlands. In 1990, WHSRN itself gave birth to Wetlands for the Americas, an organization dedicated to just such a broad-based effort to conserve the biodiversity of wetlands. In South America, however, such conservation goals must take into account the economic realities of indigenous peoples.

FACING PAGE: *Baby black oyster-catchers might well regard with apprehension their birthplace of Glacier Bay, Alaska. Such coastal environments could be altered or obliterated by the effects of global warming.* ART WOLFE

Awareness of shorebirds is being raised in South America, through the efforts of non-government organizations like Wetlands for the Americas as well as individuals. The story of the young Argentine biologist Patricia Gonzalez poignantly illustrates what can be accomplished by single-minded dedication, despite a social climate where environmentalists are often accused of being out of touch with local needs. After Gonzalez participated in a WHSRN workshop in 1988, she began to actively study the concentrations of shorebirds near her hometown of San Antonio Oeste in northern Patagonia. The extensive mud flats attract 100,000 shorebirds of seventeen species, including some 40,000 red knots, 25 per cent of the flyway population. Gonzalez became concerned for the welfare of the overwintering birds when, in the late 1980s, construction resumed on a Solvay processing plant to produce soda ash, which she feared would contaminate the feeding grounds.

Many of the 15,000 residents, understandably, wanted the construction jobs associated with the plant in this isolated area of chronic unemployment. Gonzalez had not only to battle suspicions about environmentalists but to overcome women's traditional lack of authority in her culture. "I felt totally alone," she says. Gonzalez's work was a slow process of consciousness raising for government officers and local people.

In the end, the site was declared a Provincial Protected Area by the Province of Rio Negro in June 1993, and Gonzalez herself is helping to draw up a protection plan. The area has also been designated a WHSRN international reserve. "Shorebirds unite people," Gonzalez told delegates from all thirty-one WHSRN sites when they assembled in Ottawa in May 1995 to celebrate WHSRN's tenth anniversary and to renew the mandate of wetland conservation.

WESTERN HEMISPHERE SHOREBIRD RESERVE NETWORK SITES

Kachemak Bay
Copper River Delta
Grays Harbor — Boundary Bay
Stillwater
Mono Lake
San Francisco Bay
The Grasslands
Quivira
Estero Rio Colorado
Salt Plains
Marismas Nacionales — Brazoria
Bolivar Flats

Last Mountain Lake
Quill Lakes
Benton Lake
Bay of Fundy
Great Salt Lake
Delaware Bay
Maryland / Virginia Barrier Islands
Cheyenne Bottoms
Cape Romain

Bigi Pan — Coppename
Wia-Wia
Maranhao

Paracas

Laguna Mar Chiquita — Lagoa do Peixe

San Antonio Oeste

Tierra del Fuego

WHSRN Sites

● HEMISPHERIC
hosts > 500,000 shorebirds or
30% of a flyway population

○ proposed hemispheric site

■ INTERNATIONAL
hosts > 100,000 shorebirds or
15% of a flyway population

▲ REGIONAL
hosts > 20,000 shorebirds or
5% of a flyway population

The Western Hemisphere Shorebird Reserve Network (WHSRN) protects a chain of critical habitats that shorebirds rely on during different phases of their annual cycle. The network has grown to encompass thirty-two sites in seven countries, protecting 30 million shorebirds and about 5 million hectares (12 million acres) of wetlands.

With permission of the Western Hemisphere Shorebird Reserve Network.

GLOBAL CITIZENS

Each summer, when I sit beside the Bay of Fundy entranced by the great flocks of sandpipers writing their living calligraphy across the sky, the mystery and beauty of this spectacle is enlarged further by the thought that I share this sublime experience with other birdwatchers at sister reserves, in Suriname, 4000 kilometres (2500 miles) away.

I am heartened by the thought that as peoples we are also joined in an effort to save the birds' special wetlands. The birds' migrations connect me to the great Amazon River, which unfurls its rich sediment plumes along the north coast of the southern continent; and the Suriname bird-lover is connected to the great tides of the Bay of Fundy in my backyard, which twice daily unmask their generous muds. Because of the links forged by these unprepossessing birds, I am more of a global citizen.

By protecting shorebirds, we also preserve our own capacity for wonder, an ability to see beyond the shores of our own experience. To do so, however, we must alter our definition of home to include the needs of the creatures with whom we share lakeshore, slough, and coastal beach. The strident calls of the willet, circling the salt marshes of my shorebird summers, are a declaration of its equal rights to this place. Its wing flash as it alights on the marsh is the greeting offered between respectful neighbours. May we accept these gestures with equal good faith, forging links not only with the birds but with the people with whom we share their affecting presence.

FACING PAGE: *Wilson's phalaropes, like this one doubled by its own reflection, are protected by the "twinning" of sister reserves throughout its range, under the auspices of the Western Hemisphere Shorebird Reserve Network.* DAVID WEINTRAUB

FOR FURTHER READING

Alerstam, T. 1993. *Bird Migration.* Cambridge: Cambridge University Press.

Bent, A.C. 1962. *Life Histories of North American Shore Birds.* Parts 1 and 2. New York: Dover Publications.

Bodsworth, F. 1982. *Last of the Curlews.* Toronto: McClelland & Stewart.

Burger, J., and B.L. Olla, eds. 1984. *Behavior of Marine Animals.* Vol. 5, *Shorebirds: Breeding Behavior and Populations.* New York: Plenum Press.

Burger, J., and B.L. Olla, eds. 1984. *Behavior of Marine Animals.* Vol. 6, *Shorebirds: Migration and Foraging Behavior.* New York: Plenum Press.

Cogswell, H.L. 1977. *Water Birds of California.* Berkeley: University of California Press.

Erlich, P.R., et al. 1988. *The Birder's Handbook: A Field Guide to the Natural History of North American Birds.* New York: Simon & Schuster.

Erlich, P.R., et al. 1992. *Birds in Jeopardy: The Imperilled and Extinct Birds of the United States and Canada, including Hawaii and Puerto Rico.* Stanford, Cal.: Stanford University Press.

Hale, W.G. 1981. *Waders.* London: William Collins Sons & Co.

Hayman, P., J. Marchant, and T. Prater. 1986. *Shorebirds: An Identification Guide to the Waders of the World.* Boston: Houghton Mifflin Company.

Hudson, W.H. 1945. *Far Away and Long Ago.* London: J.M. Dent & Sons.

Johnsgard, P.A. 1981. *The Plovers, Sandpipers, and Snipes of the World.* Lincoln: University of Nebraska Press.

Keast, A., and E.S. Morton, eds. 1980. *Migrant Birds in the Neotropics: Ecology, Behavior, Distribution, and Conservation.* Washington: Smithsonian Institution Press.

Leopold, A. 1991. *A Sand County Almanac.* New York: Ballantine Books.

MacKenzie, J.P.S. 1977. *Birds in Peril: A Guide to the Endangered Birds of Canada and the United States.* Toronto: McGraw-Hill Ryerson.

Matthiessen, P. 1994. *The Wind Birds: Shorebirds of North America.* Shelburne: Chapters Publishing.

Paulson, D. 1992. *Shorebirds of the Pacific Northwest.* Vancouver: University of British Columbia Press.

Pitelka, F. , ed. 1979. *Shorebirds in Marine Environments.* Studies in Avian Biology No. 2. Los Angeles: University of California / Cooper Ornithological Society.

Tuck, L.M. 1972. *The Snipes: A Study of the Genus Capella.* Canadian Wildlife Service Monograph Series No. 5. Ottawa: Environment Canada.

Williams, T.T. 1991. *Refuge: An Unnatural History of Family and Place.* New York: Pantheon Books.

INDEX